WHO KILLED LIBERAL ISLAM

WHO KILLED LIBERAL ISLAM

HASAN SUROOR

Published by
Rupa Publications India Pvt. Ltd 2019
7/16, Ansari Road, Daryaganj
New Delhi 110002

Sales Centres:
Allahabad Bengaluru Chennai
Hyderabad Jaipur Kathmandu
Kolkata Mumbai

Copyright © Hasan Suroor 2019

The views and opinions expressed in this book are the author's own and the facts are as reported by him/her which have been verified to the extent possible, and the publishers are not in any way liable for the same.

All rights reserved.
No part of this publication may be reproduced, transmitted, or stored in a retrieval system, in any form or by any means, electronic, mechanical, photocopying, recording or otherwise, without the prior permission of the publisher.

ISBN: 978-93-5333-593-9

First impression 2019

10 9 8 7 6 5 4 3 2 1

Printed at Replika Press Pvt. Ltd, India

The moral right of the author has been asserted.

This book is sold subject to the condition that it shall not, by way of trade or otherwise, be lent, resold, hired out, or otherwise circulated, without the publisher's prior consent, in any form of binding or cover other than that in which it is published.

Liberalism is a lonely, moral stance.

—Martin Luther King, Jr

CONTENTS

Islam at a Glance   *ix*
Introduction   *xiii*

PART ONE
1. The Identity Trap   3
2. Who Is a Liberal Muslim?   10
3. 'Old' Liberals vs 'New' Liberals   43
4. Liberal Roots of Indian Islam   53
5. How Liberal Islam Lost the Battle   63
6. Trapped in Mental Ghettos   79
7. Secular Islam Is a Fantasy   93
8. Why Are Young Muslims Leaving Islam   105
9. At the Bottom of the Heap   117
10. Let Us Stop Being So Boring and Pious   126

PART TWO

View From The Ground   135

1. Only Judiciary Can Initiate Reforms   136
2. Liberally Speaking...   140
3. Every Drop Contributes to the Ocean   143
4. To Hyphenate Or Not Is the Question   146
5. A Reassessment of Theology Is the Need of the Hour   151
6. Bring Multiplicity and Plurality Back   158
7. Openness Is the Key   165
8. The Closed Door of Ijtihad Needs To Be Opened   168
9. Islam Has Been Hijacked by Extremists   173

Conclusion   177
Postscript   185
Appendix 1: In the Words of a Practising Muslim Woman   201
Appendix 2: Straight Talk   203
Appendix 3: Listen to Saner Voices on Muslim Law Reform   207
Appendix 4: Beyond Mullahs and Marxists   212
Appendix 5: Islam and Its Interpretations   218
Recommended Reading   225
Acknowledgements   229
Index   231

ISLAM AT A GLANCE

ORIGINS

Founded in the seventh century CE by Prophet Mohammad after he received divine revelations from Allah, it is the youngest monotheistic religion. It is based on the belief that there is only one God, and that Mohammad is the messenger of God.

The word Islam literally means surrender (to the will of Allah.) Islam originated in Mecca and Medina and gradually spread across Arabia and beyond.

MUSLIMS IN NUMBERS

For all the negative perceptions and controversies that surround

Islam, it is the world's second largest—and fastest growing—religion with approximately 1.8 billion followers spread across seven cultural and geographical regions. Nearly a quarter of the world is Muslim. By 2050, Islam is predicted to catch up with Christianity worldwide, according to Pew Research Center.

India is home to 180 million Muslims making them the world's third largest Muslim community. Indonesia is the largest Muslim-majority country, followed by Pakistan. Only 20 per cent of the global Muslim population lives in the the Middle East where Islam was founded. The West has a large Muslim diaspora, and despite widespread Islamophobia, their number is growing.

SUNNI-SHIA DIVIDE

There are two broad segments in Islam: Sunnis and Shias, and most Muslims belong to one of the two. Sunnis are the dominant group representing almost 90 per cent of Muslims. Islam's holiest sites—Mecca and Medina—are controlled by Sunnis.

Iran is the largest Shia-majority country followed by Iraq.

The Shia-Sunni rift is the biggest and longest-running divide in Islam, going back to its early years. But the origins of this division is so arcane that, let alone non-Muslims, even many ordinary Muslims struggle to explain it.

What started off as a succession feud after Prophet Mohammad's death has come to define Islam for the modern world, thanks to the geopolitical dimensions it has taken, with a

Shia-Iran and a Sunni-Saudi Arabia competing for the leadership of the Muslim world. And both have their respective Big Power patrons—the Saudi-Sunni alliance is backed by America, and Iran by Russia. A rather obscure centuries-old religious rift has become a convenient peg on which to hang 'today's many disasters in the Middle East,' according to British academic John McHugo in his book, *Concise History of Sunnis and Shi'is*.

SHARIA

In Arabic, the term literally means path; path to water or the way to a watering hole—guiding nomadic people to a source of drinking water in the desert.

But after the advent of Islam, its followers started using it in the sense of a guide to law and morality. Broadly, it has come to mean Islamic law derived mainly from the Quran, the Sunna (the actions and authentic sayings of Prophet Mohammad), Ijma (consensus of legal scholars), and Qiyas (analogical reasoning.)

It is often described as God's Law and considered immutable by conservative Muslims. But liberals question the divine status accorded to Sharia. According to renowned liberal Islamic scholar Ziauddin Sardar, 'Sharia is not a Quranic concept' and the term occurs only twice in the Quran as a reference to 'guidance that God has provided to all nations and communities through His prophets... In neither case can we infer that the term Sharia represents a codified canon of unchanging law designed to exist for all time.' (*Reading The Quran*, Ziauddin Sardar)

The interpretation of Sharia has long been the subject of a divisive debate between traditionalists and reformists. Historically, Sharia was interpreted by muftis and their opinions (fatwas) were taken into account by judges appointed by the rulers of the day. In modern times, Sharia-based criminal laws have been incorporated into Western-inspired secular laws, with Sharia being restricted to family laws variously called Personal Status Laws and Muslim Personal Law.

Militant Islamists such as the Islamic State, Taliban, and al-Qaeda want a return to 'pure Sharia,' including reinstatement of stoning for adultery though there is no mention of stoning in the Quran. In India, Muslim opposition to changes to the Muslim Personal Law hinges on fears that it is an attempt to undermine Sharia.

IMPORTANT RITUALS

1. *Shahadah*–A profession of faith.
2. *Salat*–Prayer five times daily.
3. *Zakat*–Alms giving.
4. *Sawm*–Fasting.
5. *Hajj*–Pilgrimage to the Holy city of Mecca.

INTRODUCTION

In my last book, *India's Muslim Spring: Why Is Nobody Talking About It?* I quoted a Hindu friend telling me that the idea of a liberal Indian Muslim was a 'misnomer.'

'I have yet to meet a devout Muslim who doesn't have fundamentalist views. And mind you, I'm 70-plus and have known at least three generations of Muslims,' he said while profusely apologizing for his bluntness.

Even to me—a strong critic of Muslim fundamentalism—his remarks sounded too much like a sweeping generalization about a 180 million-strong diverse community. And had I not known him as well as I did—a progressive man and a Muslim well-wisher—I would have suspected him of anti-Muslim prejudice and stereotyping. Indeed, some readers accused me of providing a platform to Islamophobic voices; some even suggested I had made up the quote to 'sex up' the text. But, come to think of it, he was not really way off the mark. Where he was wrong was in portraying all devout Muslims as fundamentalists, but he was dead right in lamenting a dearth of liberal Muslims. A liberal Indian Muslim is indeed a rarity, judged by the generally accepted standards of liberalism—a respect for human rights, free speech, dissent, tolerance of individual freedoms and lifestyle choices, gender equality, etc.

The frequently asked question, 'Is there such a thing as a liberal Indian Muslim at all?' is a legitimate one to ask despite its offensive and provocative tone. Muslims, including many moderates, though, remain in denial. There are few things that irritate them more than being asked about the crisis of liberalism in the community. Almost reflexively, they become defensive, calling it an attempt at stereotyping them. A familiar line is that liberal Muslim voices are deliberately suppressed to create a perception that there are no liberal Muslims. The media in particular is seen as the chief villain with its penchant for playing up controversial fundamentalist views in the garb of news. As a media person, I admit there is a bias but it is not so much about wilfully suppressing liberal voices as about playing up potentially headline grabbing views. Simply because controversy sells. That is the nature of the beast: it thrives on sensationalism.

For the moment, let us take at face value the Muslim denial that the community suffers from a crisis of liberalism, and run a reality check. So, who are these liberal Muslims that it is supposed to be teeming with? And how representative are they of the wider Muslim society? How much influence do they wield on fellow Muslims? And are they numerous and influential enough to swing opinion in favour of reforms? These are important questions but have been swept aside in an increasingly polarized debate in which all Muslims are either versions of mad mullahs (as in my friend's version), or all bleeding-heart liberals as implied in the defensive Muslim reaction. The whole issue has been reduced to competing extreme narratives depending on which side of the divide you are on.

This book is an attempt to bring some perspective to the debate by challenging the self-serving claims of both sides of the aisle. But my specific aim is to lay bare the reality behind the generally touted notion of a liberal Muslim and his/her supposed clout in the wider community. In particular, I question the authenticity of the kind of Muslims who are commonly presented as the liberal and progressive public face of the community. Yes, they are liberals, but Muslims? The fact is that they simply happen to be Muslims. Most of them have about as much to do with Islam or the Muslim community, as champagne socialists with socialism.

SO, WHO ARE THEY?

To borrow Jean Paul Sartre's description of self-loathing Jews, they can be classed as 'inauthentic' Muslims: a small English-speaking urban elite of mostly left-wing, non-practising Muslims (many of them even atheists) with the most tenuous of links with the mainstream community. Their grounding in Islam and understanding of Islamic issues happen to be even more superficial. To be fair, they themselves make no claims about their religiosity. On the contrary, they proudly flaunt their aversion to religion and barely conceal their impatience with people proclaiming the faith. This group looks down upon them as ignorant and regressive.

Towards the wider Muslim community, their attitude is one of a mixture of condescension and contempt. The community, in turn, has no love lost for them and regards them with as much suspicion and contempt. They are seen as 'outsiders' who are not to be trusted as honest brokers. The liberals' tactless approach that includes aggressive secularism and sweeping criticism of Muslims who are not like them, has alienated the moderates as well. Anyone who has ever heard self-proclaimed atheists like Javed Akhtar or Naseeruddin Shah lecture conservative Muslims, would have noted their patronizing tone—something that even those broadly in agreement with their views find irritating. I would, if I were them.

The central point the book seeks to make is that the left-wing Muslim intellectuals paraded as the community's beating liberal heart—the Muslims who write op-ed pieces and appear on TV to denounce Sharia—have in fact done more damage to the cause of Muslim liberalism than good. They are not agents of change. On the contrary, by coming across as confrontational and hostile, they have the effect of undermining the few moderates in the community who are trying to bring about change.

And here is a confession: I too was once a part of this cabal of self-styled modernizers. Until the penny dropped and I realized how delusional I had been in believing that a faith-baiting liberal would be embraced by a deeply religious and socially conservative community. Imagine a serial sinner wanting to run a seminary and expecting to be taken seriously!

Let us flip the situation around: what if a liberal-baiting mullah were to come along expecting the liberals to hug him? Will the liberals take him seriously? I argue that the role of Left liberals in weakening the pushback against fundamentalists has not only not received enough attention, it has gone almost unnoticed. It is time to hold them to account for their back-handed approach.

At this point, readers could legitimately ask: So what's the right approach? To which the answer is: For starters, stop treating 180 million Muslims as a fundamentalist monolith. Because they are not. The fact is that contrary to the popular perception, the community is largely moderate. There are Muslims who may not answer to the Oxford Dictionary's description of a liberal, but may strongly believe in change and the need for the community to modernize. Some are even quietly working to bring it about. These are mostly young practising Muslims who, despite their fixation with Islamic symbols of identity (most wear hijab or have beard), are refreshingly modern, open-minded and secular.

If I were a gambling type, I would put my money on these Muslims—not on left-wing liberals—as drivers of change. For the simple reason that they have the insiders advantage and approach issues from a Muslim perspective, as against the Left liberals' secular viewpoint. As an integral part of the community they have a better sense of its disposition and how far it is prepared to move forward. They are aware of the limits of the community's appetite for reforms. More importantly, the community sees them as their own (as against ideological zealots seeking to impose reforms from above), and is therefore more willing to listen to them. They have street cred that Left liberals sorely lack.

Meanwhile, a fact often lost in the din of a polarized debate is that except for the mullahs, whose size and influence has been grossly exaggerated by the way, most mainstream Muslims are not opposed to reforms. What they *are* opposed to is any attempt to impose changes on them—and to be presented with a *fait accompli*. They are suspicious of any hint of outside interference either by the state or individuals who they regard as outsiders. And high on their list are posh liberals whether Muslim or Hindu, particularly Muslims of the type I have just described.

I believe that the job of reforming Indian Islam is best left to those who are better equipped and better placed to do it—the moderates within the community. And instead of dismissing them as 'soft fundamentalists,' we should support them in the very difficult task they are trying to do in a challenging environment. It must be remembered that India has a long history of Muslim reformers who were deeply religious (the sort our Left liberal set would have turned their noses at), and in fact used religion to sell their reforms—Sir Syed Ahmed, Zakir Husain and Abul Kalam

INTRODUCTION

Azad, just to mention a few household names. I devote a whole chapter to these pioneering home-grown reformists who didn't allow their religiosity to stand in the way of progress.

While the focus of my book is on Indian Muslims, I also look at the broader global debate over liberalizing Islam. Drawing on historical debates and writings, I contest the routinely made claim that a historically liberal and tolerant religion has been 'suddenly' hijacked by extremists, and show how, in fact, Islam lost to the hardliners very early in its history. Sporadic attempts to revive it haven't worked. It is notable that there has been a backlash whenever reformists have sought to railroad reforms and push them before the community was actually ready for them. It is a warning to impatient Indian secularists seeking sweeping reforms overnight.

Citing research, I contend that claims relating to Islam as a peaceful religion are based on a cherry-picked reading of Islam's chequered history, ignoring its history of violence, intolerance, repression and cruelty as rival schools of thought competed for supremacy and patronage of the ruler of the day. Three successive Caliphs—Umar, Uthman, and Ali—were assassinated in a long and bloody battle for succession. Islam's subsequent history as it spread across the world was also marked by violence and repression. No doubt, like all religions, Islam too is inherently peaceful and preaches tolerance and co-existence. It was founded on the principles of equality and justice and was considered quite revolutionary at the time, but like all revolutions it lost its way in its quest for supremacy.

WHERE DOES IT GO FROM HERE?

In order to answer this question we first need to clear the confusion around what we mean by 'modernizing' Islam. This confusion has led to two very different aspects of Islam to be conflated. Thus, there is a tendency to speak about 'secular' Islam and 'liberal' Islam in the same breath, with one being substituted for the other. They are presented as two sides of the same coin. But I argue that they are not, and it is important to understand the distinction between the two. Because, while Islam is open to liberalization, a secular Islam is a fantasy.

Turkey's Kemal Ataturk and the Shah of Iran chose the secularization path to modernizing Islam by literally banishing it from public life altogether. And look what happened: Islam is back with a bang in both countries—the result of a backlash which might have taken some time to kick in, but it is a warning to our own reformists who confuse modernization with secularization.

It is important to understand why the idea of secularism is incompatible with Islam's inherent all-pervasive philosophy. In other words, Islam doesn't recognize that there is any such thing as a secular public space; Islam is ubiquitous. It is said that if you are a Muslim, the religion has something to say to you every second of your life—right from personal habits to food choices.

But contrary to what the fundamentalists might claim, Islam is not resistant to specific reforms if it can be done by shedding or tweaking practices that no longer fit the purpose.

INTRODUCTION

Such reforms have already occurred in a number of Muslim countries, and Indian Muslims can take a cue from them. It will require some hard decisions, but it is doable if there is a will to do it. I believe that Indian Muslims remain overwhelmingly moderate—conservative but not fanatical, and under the right kind of leadership, they can be won over and Indian Islam restored to its tolerant heritage. But it will not be easy and the task is made more difficult by the rising tide of right-wing Hindu nationalism which, besides fuelling Muslim fundamentalism, has put even moderate Muslims on the defensive. In the current political climate, 'achhe din' for Muslim reforms look far off.

Since the crisis of liberalism in Indian Islam cannot be looked at in isolation from what is happening in the wider global 'umma', the book offers an overview of the issues of democratic legitimacy and socio-educational backwardness in the Islamic world, citing UN Human Development reports and informed commentators.

Finally, Muslims from across the spectrum define liberalism in their own words and what it means to be a Muslim today. Because of its association with Western political and cultural hegemony, liberalism has always been a contentious issue in the non-Western world, particularly in the more conservative Asian and Middle Eastern societies. And, of course, Islam has its own particular problem with the idea of free-wheeling individualism that liberalism has come to imply. But, like it or not, it is also the only antidote against the growing culture of hate and intolerance—of which, by the way, minorities are the worst victims, as Muslims so well know.

My intention in writing this book is to help concentrate Muslim minds on an issue that they have sought to avoid discussing mostly on flimsy grounds. It is time to at least start a serious debate and see where it goes. Is that too much to ask for without being seen as pushing an Islamophobic agenda?

London
April 2019

Part One

Part One

1
THE IDENTITY TRAP

Let me start with a fictional scenario which may sound a bit silly but is not entirely without precedent. Besides, I have lived long enough and experienced rather a lot to realize that the line between fiction and reality is not as clear-cut as we wish to believe. So, here it goes:

Imagine that by an unlikely quirk of fate, Indian Muslims find themselves stranded on a desert island with no prospect of being rescued. Faced with the task of building a new community or society from scratch, what kind of society will they seek to build? A liberal and secular one? Or one shaped by the idea of Muslim 'identity'? And if they were to stumble upon some non-Muslim native settlers, how would the Muslims treat them? As equal partners in building a diverse community? Or as infidels?

Which way they swing in such circumstances—choose faith as the building block of a new Muslim-majority community, or take the liberal and secular path—will be the test of Indian Muslim liberalism.

Historical precedents of Muslim majority behaviour are not promising. It is faith, the idea of Muslim brotherhood, and an overwhelming sense of Muslim superiority that have won most of the time. And I would be surprised if my fictional lot of Muslims would behave any different. Over time, the imaginary island will transform into an Islamic Republic of sorts.

It is not that all Muslims are closet fundamentalists waiting to impose Sharia on the rest of the world. It is the nature of Islamic faith. The sense of being a Muslim is simply too overwhelming to resist by even non-practising or liberal Muslims. Islam is not just a religion—it is a vast smothering brotherhood, and it sucks you in whatever your private views may be. Willy-nilly you become part of it. There is a seductive charm about being part of a global community bound by a common faith and rituals. And Islamic rituals—namaaz congregations, Hajj, Ramzan—were designed to create this sense of Muslim identity that subsumes all other identities.

Asra Nomani, a well-known American Muslim journalist of Indian origin, who says she had zero knowledge of Islam and 'never felt a connection to the Muslim community,' suddenly felt connected to the global Muslim ummah when she went on a Hajj pilgrimage out of sheer curiosity and to write about it for an American journal. She writes that she was overwhelmed by a sense of community the moment she landed at the Jeddah airport amid a 'sea' of fellow pilgrims from all parts of the world.

> My father looked around in awe. "This," he said, "is ummah." Ummah? I didn't understand what the word meant. My father explained that it meant community...with awe, I looked at the diversity in front of me. It was a window for me into the breadth of the Muslim ummah, and I was struck by its plurality. What I saw was people who were very different from each other coming together for a common purpose... On the Hajj we were equalized by what we wore: the men were cloaked in the same seamless white fabrics, and the women in simple clothes.
>
> (*Standing Alone in Mecca: A Pilgrimage into the Heart of Islam*, Asra Nomani)

All religions have rituals that bring their followers together, but the spirit of communitarianism that Islam seeks to foster, is unique in its intensity. It almost doesn't recognize any identity outside the ummah. Being a Muslim comes first. So, when Muslims are thrown together, they instinctively wind up forming a bond that excludes all others. Non-Muslims are seen as gate-crashers.

THE CULTURAL MUSLIM

Pakistan was founded not by thuggish mullahs but an educated and mostly liberal and secular elite, on grounds that they may not get a fair treatment in a Hindu-majority India. Mohammed Ali Jinnah projected it as a replica of the Indian model, with freedom of worship and equal rights for all, irrespective of one's faith. In his address to Pakistan's Constituent Assembly on 11 August, 1947, he emphatically invoked the vision of a secular State in which every citizen would be free to follow his or her own religion. The State, he declared, shall make no distinction on the basis of their faith.

Ostensibly, Pakistan was conceived as a secular, liberal and democratic State with no reference to Islam—a view endorsed by many leading historians like Ayesha Jalal (*The Sole Spokesman: Jinnah, the Muslim League, and the Demand for Pakistan*) And, indeed, initially this is how it was—'no Sharia, no clerics, no ban on alcohol; people remember women on bicycles'—as Aatish Taseer writes in his book, *Stranger to History: A Son's Journey Through Muslim Lands*.

But soon enough the long arm of 'Muslimness' caught up with Pakistan, consigning Jinnah's vision to the dustbin of history. Bangladesh's transformation from a child of revolution to a playground of Islamists is even more egregious. At the heart of it all is the irresistible pull of identity which sweeps aside all other impulses. In her book, *Making Sense of Pakistan*, Pakistani historian Farzana Shaikh has written incisively about the tension between the collective Muslim sense of identity and their individual liberal impulses as illustrated by the failure of Jinnah's original vision.

Aatish Taseer cites the case of his own father, Salman Taseer, the liberal Pakistani politician who was killed by his bodyguard in 2011 because of his opposition to the country's blasphemy law. He was not a practising Muslim and liked to describe himself as a 'cultural Muslim.' Yet, he saw himself as a defender of the faith and felt himself a part of Muslim or Islamic history. He hated Jews and used anti-Semitic tropes to denounce them, stopping just short of questioning the Holocaust. He also shared some of the 9/11 conspiracy theories that cast doubts about the extent of Muslim involvement in the attack.

Hindus, he thought were 'weak' even though he had been briefly married to a Hindu journalist Tavleen Singh and had many Hindu admirers in India. Glories of Islamic past apparently excited him no end, and he didn't brook any criticism of either his faith (though he himself didn't believe in it), or the wider Muslim brotherhood. He fell out with his son after he wrote a critical piece about Britain's Pakistani Muslims following the 7 July, 2005 terror attack on the London Underground which was masterminded by a group of Muslims of Pakistani origin.

Asked by his son what it meant to be a 'cultural Muslim,' he replied: 'You see it all around you. Everyone I know is Muslim. You see namaaz (prayers), and rozas (fasts), all the servants are Muslim, and with Islam, people believe deeply. It happens that I don't privately, but I wouldn't dream of criticizing Islam.'

Aatish Taseer's verdict on his father's liberalism is this:

> ...I felt sure that none of Islam's once powerful moral imperatives existed within him, but he was a Muslim because he doubted the Holocaust, hated America and Israel, thought Hindus were weak and cowardly, and because the glories of the Islamic past excited him. The faith decayed within him, ceased to be dynamic, ceased to provide moral guidance, *became nothing but a deep, unreachable historical and political identity.*' (italics mine)

Salman Taseer typified the liberal 'cultural Muslim': having nothing to do with the faith but still weighed down by the sheer force of Muslim or Islamic identity. He was the embodiment of a South Asian liberal Muslim—who is neither a Muslim, nor a liberal. There is a Salman Taseer in every ostensibly liberal Muslim: our liberalism (yes, I include myself among them) is, in the end, defeated by a compelling sense of our Muslim identity which we believe makes us unique vis-a-vis others.

Deep down, all Muslims harbour fears about attempts to undermine their identity—sources of threat ranging from the Hindu Right and the Far Left, to Jews and the Christian West. This fear binds the umma together.

Indian Muslim community is full of these cultural Muslims for whom being Muslim boils down to Friday prayers (not even that for many); Eid; and saying *Inshallah* and *Mashallah* on appropriate occasions. They take pride in their liberalism—they drink, they party, some even marry non-Muslims though most men insist on converting their partner to Islam, and they make no pretence of their disdain for religion. But, crucially, they never forget that they are Muslim. Not only that, like Salman Taseer, they fancy themselves as keepers of the faith and are quick to take offence at even well-meaning criticism of Islam—or Muslims. That is how deeply embedded the idea of identity is. It never lets go of you. Remember the famous 1970s Hotel California lyric: 'You can check out any time you like, But you can never leave!'

2

WHO IS A LIBERAL MUSLIM?

In the autumn of 2017, a mosque in Berlin witnessed an extraordinary scene variously hailed as an act of bravery and a stunt. An Algerian-German Islamic scholar called Abdel Hakim Ourghi, nailed '40 Theses'—a manifesto of reforms to bring Islam into modernity—on the door of the mosque. It was a re-enactment of the famous '95 Theses' that Martin Luther, the reformist German Catholic monk, had nailed to the door of a church in Wittenberg half a millennium ago, setting in motion a revolution in the Catholic Church.

Ourghi, who teaches Islamic theology at the University of Freiburg and is one of the founders of a liberal mosque in Berlin, said, 'I'm asking: what Islam do we need in Germany? And my answer is: one that is humanist and moderate, one that can be reformed. It is the task of liberal Muslims to reform our religion.' The reforms included a radical 'reinterpretation' of the Quran ('The Koran is lifeless, only its interpretation makes it come alive.') and more freedom for Muslim women who, he said, were being treated like 'slaves.'

It is hard to imagine a similar protest by a liberal Muslim in India. I'm not even sure how many would come out to support such a person in the unlikely event of someone taking the plunge. Or if there is even such a thing as a liberal Muslim?

It is a provocative question and generally posed by Muslim-baiters. But, surprisingly, I first heard it from Muslims themselves in Aligarh Muslim University (AMU) way back in the 1980s, when it was captured by a politically influential cabal of right-wing Muslim groups who promptly set about 'Islamizing' the university and targeting liberal faculty members as well as students. I had gone there to report on the incident for *The Statesman,* and I remember asking some teachers why wasn't there a liberal Muslim reaction to the fundamentalist attempts to destroy AMU's famed secular character.

They gave me a look of bewilderment and asked, 'Are you serious? Do you really believe in the idea of a liberal Muslim? Wake up, man.' I am, of course, paraphrasing what they said in Urdu. But such is the general perception even in a so-called secular space as AMU. Later, a colleague was told by a prominent Muslim left-wing AMU academic that the term 'liberal Muslim' was a contradiction in terms. 'You're either a liberal or a Muslim.

Can't be both,' he had reportedly said. As it was an off-the-record conversation, I am not at liberty to disclose his name.

That was a rare admission, even if it was meant as a joke. The default Muslim response to the question: 'why is there such a dearth of liberal Muslims,' is exactly the opposite. It is to get into a full-on defensive mode, angrily rejecting the suggestion that Muslims are not liberal and accuse the questioner of nursing an anti-Islam bias.

'Of course there are plenty of liberal Muslims but nobody wants to notice them,' they complain. But when you ask them their definition of a liberal Muslim, they clam up. The biggest problem I had in writing this book was getting a straight answer to the questions: Who is a liberal Muslim? And are there enough of them to make a difference?

Such questions make most Muslims extremely suspicious; they see it as an attempt to box them into binaries of liberal/illiberal and good/bad Muslims. The issue is so sensitive that several prominent self-described liberal Muslims declined to be interviewed, presumably to avoid controversy. Some pulled out citing sudden illness or workload, one high-profile figure said it was not fair to look at a large and diverse community in 'black and white/either or terms.' Some argued that the idea of an 'all-weather' liberal was a bit silly. A person could take different positions in different situations. 'Depends on the context,' they say. For example, a Muslim woman might take a liberal position on gender equality and equal rights for women under Sharia, but then not be so liberal when it comes to—for instance—allowing her daughter the right to wear what she likes, or marry whoever she wishes.. How would you describe her? Liberal or illiberal?

Frankly, it sounds like a lot of quibbling to me. After all, there *is* a widely accepted broad definition of liberalism which includes open-mindedness, tolerance, freedom of thought, individual liberty, critical thinking, inclusion, rule of law, gender equality, pluralism, democracy, secularism, *et al*. And then, there is the Oxford English Dictionary definition of a 'theological liberal' (a religious person with a liberal outlook) as one who regards 'many traditional beliefs as dispensable, invalidated by modern thought, or liable to change.' In other words, someone who gives precedence to reason and rational thought over dogma and orthodoxy; who accepts that traditional beliefs are not sacrosanct or written in stone, but open to reconsideration if the situation or the context demands it.

Muslims, however, believe that the Islamic doctrine is immutable. It is a deeply held belief particularly among practising Muslims. Thus, the Quran and Sharia are strictly no-go areas and any suggestion that they need a fresh look is seen as an attempt to interfere with divine laws.

'Sharia is the biggest obstacle to change,' according to historian S. Irfan Habib. This, despite the fact that the Quran is only one of its four sources along with *Qiyas* (human reasoning), *Ijma* (consensus) and *Sunnah* (sayings of the Prophet), most of which were written some 200 years after the Prophet's death and many having no authenticity. A number of practices justified in the name of Sharia, have no Quranic sanctions.

> For example, the Quran does not mention stoning adulterers to death, killing apostates, or throwing homosexuals from tall buildings. *Nor does it mention men growing their beards ...or women (from) covering their hair* (italics mine.) All these actions are derived from alleged sayings of the Prophet. Muslims have lost the courage to question hadiths that do not align with the Quran.
>
> *(The House of Islam: A Global History, Ed Husain)*

Indian Muslims, certainly, have. Rare is a Muslim who will countenance criticism of Sharia or the Prophet. Note the deafening silence over blasphemy and apostasy—both of which are punishable by death in many Islamic countries, including Pakistan. Their liberalism is heavily constrained by their rigid belief in the divine nature of Islamic scriptures, and the infallibility of the Prophet, though he himself never claimed exemption from criticism. Indeed, he was a keen listener and extremely receptive to public opinion. He listened, he debated and he strove to understand the opposite viewpoint. He was constantly aware of his own fallibility and, I quote:

> ...everyday he begged God to forgive his own failings and oversights... He loved, he forgave... and when a man or a woman came to him burdened with a mistake, however serious, he received that soul and showed her or him the way to forgiveness...
>
> *(The Messenger: The Meanings of the Life of Muhammad, Tariq Ramadan).*

The Prophet would have been shocked that people are being hanged for allegedly insulting him. Every time someone is prosecuted in Pakistan on blasphemy charges, one expects at least a murmur of protest from self-proclaimed liberal Muslims. But there is never even a squeak. Only deafening silence. The case of Asia Bibi, a Christian Pakistani woman sentenced to death on the charge of blasphemy but later acquitted, caused outrage around the world but Muslims *everywhere* remained unmoved. In fact, the British government was so nervous about the Muslim reaction that it turned down her request for asylum. Salman Rushdie remains the most hated figure among Muslims of all stripes for 'insulting' Prophet Mohammad in his *The Satanic Verses*.

Take another burning issue: the persecution of vulnerable religious minorities. It is supposed to be the hallmark of a liberal to be instinctively empathetic towards victims of religious or racial hate, and to speak up for them. Liberal Hindus consistently stand up for Muslim victims of Hindu fanatics but it is rare for Muslims to raise their voice against the plight of non-Muslim minorities—Shias or Christians in Pakistan; Christians and Yazidis in the Middle East; or Kashmiri pandits nearer home. Let alone public protest, it is not even a topic of academic discussion in the community.

We spring into action only when other Muslims are in trouble; Muslim violence against non-Muslim minorities leaves us cold. It seems those outside the umma are not our problem. Can there be a more glaring example of 'othering' those with whom we don't feel religious affinity? It is an astonishing attitude to take for a community that itself is a victim of religious prejudice and constantly expects others to stand up for it.

But then, 'we are like that only,' to borrow the title of Rama Bijapurkar's best-seller about the quixotic behaviour of Indians, and the difficulty of making sense of it.

INTELLECTUAL TIMIDITY

For all the quibbling, the fact is that there *are* definitions of liberalism, however imperfect, and the argument that it is a nebulous concept or a trick to 'box in' Muslims into good and bad categories, doesn't hold water. You don't even need a definition to spot a liberal. It is one of those things that you can tell when you see it. There is the famous observation of an American supreme court judge, late Justice Potter Stewart, about the difficulty of defining obscenity. Presiding over a case in 1964, he said, 'I shall not today attempt further to define the kinds of material I understand to be embraced within that shorthand description [hard-core pornography]; and perhaps I could never succeed in intelligibly doing so. But I know it when I see it.'

But here is the problem: we don't 'see' Muslim liberalism. Anyone trying to look for it on the basis of any of the above definitions, including that of Potter, are likely to struggle. Take any standard measure of liberalism and Indian Muslims will flunk it.

The depth of the crisis is underlined by the fact that there is so much equivocation and hair-splitting in the community around the issue. Most Muslims, I discovered while working on this book, are reluctant to have a conversation on the subject, exposing an extraordinary intellectual timidity to confront the problem. And this intellectual faint-heartedness, in a way, lies at the heart of the crisis of liberalism among Indian Muslims, and explains why we rarely hear an honest Muslim critique of the community's many self-inflicted ills. Everything, we are told, is somebody else's fault—either stereotyped by a biased media, exploited by secular parties, or abused and intimidated by Hindu nationalists.

Ovais Sultan Khan is a young and articulate rights activist with supposedly progressive views. An interview he gave to the UK-based video media website Cine-Ink has been widely hailed for offering 'positive perspectives' about Indian Muslims, and I was strongly advised by friends to watch it. So, I did. And it was like watching a re-run of a very old film. The entire narrative, couched in polished rhetoric, was one of victimhood—exploited by 'secular' forces, hounded by RSS storm-troopers—with no mention of the community's own responsibility for the situation it finds itself in. Muslims are always right; others always wrong. Here is a sampling:

- *Question: why must calls for namaaz be broadcast through loudspeakers five times a day and disturb others?*
  Answer: But what about all-night jagrans broadcast through loudspeakers? Why doesn't anybody object to that? Why should Muslims be discriminated?

- *Question: Why offer namaaz in a public place and cause inconvenience to others?*
  Answer: What else to do, when they don't allow us to build mosques?

So low is the Muslim liberal threshold that Khan is being hailed as a future 'progressive' leader of the community! The future of liberal Muslim leadership doesn't look exactly promising.

Meanwhile, we can rail at the media all we like for stereotyping Muslims and ignoring moderate voices in favour of fatwa-spewing mullahs, but the reality is that when offered a platform, the moderates have nothing new to say, and, like the young Khan, end up sounding much like the mullahs themselves. With the exception that they don't scream and shout or abuse their critics; instead they are articulate and use sophisticated argument to justify and rationalize the most regressive ideas.

Then there are those who clam up fearing imagined hidden traps; or simply try to play safe. To be sure, speaking up has its hazards—you end up ruffling feathers, and making enemies while risking handing ammunition to critics, or to the 'other' side. There is also the notion of Muslim solidarity—you don't beat up your own side when it is already down and under attack from external forces. 'This is not the time for self-flagellation,' one friend told me. But, conversely, there is no good time to speak up either. The need for liberal intervention and leadership is the greatest in times of crisis such as the one Muslims are facing today. It is in situations like these that the liberal mettle is tested: you can either choose the path of least resistance and remain silent, and in the process come across as a bit of a wimp. Or, you can take the plunge and offer the community a credible leadership. Martin Luther King (Jr), breaking his silence over the Vietnam war despite warnings of a patriotic backlash, had said, 'A time comes when silence is betrayal.'

Unfortunately, India's liberal Muslims have chosen silence as the default option. 'It is time for them to emerge from their armchair discussions... Islamic Liberal discourse needs to play a key role. It is time for them to address Constitutional rights, individual liberty, freedom of thought and expression, rule of law, accompanied by critical thinking, the ability to transform without fear or favour. Development, advancement in ideas and progress on national and international affairs are the need of the hour,' said Zeenat Shaukat Ali, former Professor of Islamic Studies, St. Xavier's College, Mumbai, and Director General, The Wisdom Foundation.

Sometimes, it is hard to believe we are the descendants of a generation of Muslims who stood up to be counted when it mattered: in 1947 our parents and grandparents rejected narrow Muslim identity politics that led to the Partition, and instead chose to embrace pluralism even at the cost of losing family members and friends, not to mention potential career opportunities in Pakistan. Of course, this argument can be turned on its head, and it can be said that those who chose to go to Pakistan were also our ancestors. But, it is often forgotten or wilfully overlooked that a majority of Muslims *chose* to stay back in India in a massive thumbs-down to the idea of a Muslim homeland. We are the inheritors of their values. Faced with a choice between an exclusionist Muslim nationalism on the one hand, and inclusive secularism on the other, they had no doubt what was the right thing to do.

I am not suggesting that, confronted with (God forbid) a similar choice today, most Muslims would not make the right choice. Yet, there is no point pretending that the old liberal instinct remains as strong. Whatever the reasons, it has been eroded over the years and replaced by a growing obsession with Muslim identity; ironically, particularly among a new class of well-heeled practising Muslims who equate burqa and beard with 'Muslimness.' Their battle cry seems to be *Garv se kaho hum Mussalman hain* (say with pride, we're Muslim) echoing the 1990s Hindutva slogan: *Garv se kaho hum Hindu hain* (say with pride, we're Hindu.) They are the new mullahs—part of an increasing backlash against the traditional left liberal Muslims—representing a particular brand of liberalism, discussed later.

Here it is important to underline that Muslim liberalism has seen better days. Indeed, until well into the sixties there was a thriving community of liberal Muslims—journalists, writers, academics, artistes, grassroots political activists. In the 1950s, Muslim women in Old Delhi coalesced around progressive causes defying community and family pressures. The Communist Party of India's women's wing had its most active branch in the conservative Muslim ghettos of Ballimaran and Jama Masjid. They lobbied with conservative parents to educate their daughters, give them the freedom to go out on their own, not push them into early marriage, not force them to wear burqa. Naturally, they were accused of 'brainwashing' innocent girls and indulging in 'un-Islamic activities' but they persisted instead of running away from the debate. My mother was one of them; she was ostracized by conservatives for not wearing burqa and campaigning for women's rights. Sadly, today, that same area is awash with burqas and other bogus symbols of Muslim identity—and a narrative of victimhood, helplessness and hopelessness has replaced the zest for change.

Like me and many other Muslims of a certain generation, Saba Hasan, a well-known artist and an anthropologist, was a witness to an era of robust Muslim liberalism. Rebutting the narrative that Indian Muslims have no tradition of liberalism, Saba writes:

> In my family, I don't remember my grandmother wearing a *burkha* and nor did my mother or my aunts; in fact, they were among the first Indian women to get a higher education. Some went abroad for their doctorates. My grandfather was in the administrative service, he read his *namaaz* five times a day and saw that his children grew up to be scientists, doctors and journalists, like my parents, who were also politically committed. His idea of a liberal education included music, so after giving us math problems to solve, *nana abba* used to tune into his favourite Bade Ghulam Ali Khan and hum along. My introduction to art too came from within the family when I

went with my father to the National Gallery, when I was ten years old and he pointed out a Leonardo Da Vinci drawing as his favourite….

(*The Wire*, 5 August, 2017)

So, what happened?

It was somewhere circa late sixties that we lost our way, and are still struggling to find it. It coincided with the start of the decline of progressive political forces that saw the Congress and the Left displaced from their perch by proponents of identity politics built around caste and Hindu nationalism. Conservative Muslims were quick to capitalize on it to promote their own parochial agenda centred on Muslim identity. As the preservation, protection and promotion of sectarian cultural identities took centre-stage in national politics, becoming the only show in town, it didn't take long for liberal Muslims to jump on the bandwagon as well. From then on, it went steadily downhill. And soon, the Muslim Agenda was reduced to Muslim Personal Law, Aligarh Muslim University, Jamia Millia Islamia, the madrasas, the hijabs and skullcaps. What was thought at the time to be a passing phase—a response to a specific situation—has lingered on. If anything, our pre-occupation with Muslim identity has become almost obsessive. It is no longer confined to the mullahs, but has spread across the community, including self-proclaimed liberals. Even well-meaning criticism is seen as an attack on the community as a whole. This is illustrated by the following episode.

WHO IS A LIBERAL MUSLIM?

In March 2018, two of India's most respected Hindu liberal intellectuals—historian Ram Chandra Guha, and rights activist Harsh Mander—were involved in an extraordinary public spat. It was sparked by an article in *The Indian Express* (Sonia, Sadly, 17 March, 2018) by Mander arguing that there was a systematic attempt to banish Muslim symbols of identity from public space, and render them politically irrelevant—'political orphans with no home' in any political party. 'Most political parties are accepting the premise that the majority Hindu vote will sour if a party is seen to be close to Muslims. In her nineteen years of leadership of the Congress, Sonia Gandhi never faltered in her secular convictions. But when even she declared recently that the Congress suffered because the BJP persuaded people that it was a Muslim party, many Muslims felt their expulsion to the political wilderness was complete.' Then he quoted an anonymous Dalit leader telling Muslims who attended his rally: 'By all means come in large numbers to our rallies. But don't come with your skullcaps and burqas.' Muslims, he said, were being urged to 'voluntarily withdraw from politics.'

This brought forth an uncharacteristically combative response from Guha, lauding the unnamed Dalit leader for telling off Muslims who flaunted 'antediluvian' symbols of their religious-cultural identity. He wrote that Mander 'is a friend of some 40 years' standing, and on many issues we have stood on the same side' but that this time regrettably he had got it wrong. Questioning Mander's defence of burqa and skullcap, he said the fact was that they represented the 'most reactionary' and 'antediluvian' aspects of the faith.

'To object to its display in public is a mark not of intolerance, but of liberalism and emancipation (Liberals, Sadly, *The Indian Express,* 2 March, 2018) he argued.

'He (Mander) is dismayed by this (Dalit leader's) advice, seeing it as a gratuitous attempt to get Muslims to voluntarily withdraw from politics. To the contrary, while the words may be harsh and direct, the spirit of the advice was forward-looking,' he wrote. Those who objected to 'Hindus flaunting saffron robes and trishuls at rallies' but defended Muslims wearing burqa and skullcaps were guilty of hypocrisy, he suggested. While a burqa may not be a weapon, 'in a symbolic sense it is akin to a trishul.'

Guha's remarks provoked a furious reaction from across the Hindu-Muslim liberal spectrum and what had started as an exchange between two old friends ballooned into a heated debate on the broader issue of Muslim identity. Overnight, Guha, who had until then been a darling of liberal Muslims, turned from hero to zero. *Et tu Guha?* they asked in bewilderment, calling his remarks patronizing.

'Comparison of the burqa, a symbol of a besieged minority, with the trishul, a symbol of aggressive majoritarianism, is callous and insensitive,' wrote Irena Akbar, an art curator and writer, in *Why This Liberal Muslim Refuses To Be Patronised By The Liberal Hindu*, echoing a widespread Muslim reaction.

The debate played out in *The Indian Express* Op-Ed pages for several weeks with Guha getting a dressing down from across the

WHO IS A LIBERAL MUSLIM?

liberal Muslim spectrum. Admittedly, Guha went over the top in comparing hijab and skullcaps with trishul, but equally over the top was the liberal Muslim reaction. A long-standing friend and champion of minorities was suddenly cast as an Islamophobe simply because of a slightly ham-handed foray into polemic. Even an apology from him failed to calm Muslim nerves.

Is that *it* then? Was the AMU academic right who described a liberal Muslim as an oxymoron? I wouldn't go that far, but it certainly is a very elusive entity. It remains the case that a devout Muslim is more likely to be a conservative than a liberal. Some might say, 'But isn't that true of all devout people of faith irrespective of their religion?' Fair question, except that Islam—as it has evolved—has become more insular than any other mainstream faith, encouraging its followers to look at everything from an Islamic perspective, thereby leaving little room for them to develop a liberal worldview. Pluralism, the beating heart of liberalism, is not a strong point of contemporary Islam. After all, there is not a single Islamic or Muslim majority country which is democratic, secular and tolerant of non-Muslims.

Conscious of this, some Muslims reject the term 'liberal Muslim' altogether, and go to some lengths to separate their faith from the broader worldview. They told me that when asked if they would call themselves a liberal Muslim, their response is: 'I am a liberal, and I am also Muslim. There is no co-relation between the two.' But there is, as I have shown above.

To some extent, that is true of pious followers of all faiths. In the West, practising Catholics are constantly struggling to reconcile their politics with their Catholic beliefs. The notion of 'conscientious objection' is commonly invoked to oppose liberal reforms such as gay marriage or abortion, arguing that it is in conflict with their Christian faith. In 2016, the leader of the British Liberal Democratic Party, Tim Farron, resigned less than a week after his election saying he was 'torn between living as a faithful Christian and serving as a political leader.'

'To be a leader, particularly of a progressive liberal party in 2017 and to live as a committed Christian and to hold faithful to the Bible's teaching, has felt impossible for me,' he said, particularly referring to a controversy over his reluctance to endorse gay sex. De-hyphenating liberal and Islam will not change the fact that a practising Muslim cannot escape the influence of his or her Islamic beliefs. Like Tim Farron, their fealty to their faith comes first. So, let us stick to the hyphen.

But now to the most curious part of the liberal Muslim story. The story of how some of the most 'un-Muslim' Muslims have become the public liberal face of the community. They are always popping up in television studios and on Op-Ed pages, dissecting the Muslim community's ills and prescribing remedies. The fact, though, is that they are about as representative of India's 180-million Muslim community as its fundamentalist fringe. Their Muslimness is deeply contested, and their brand of liberalism is way out of sync with the community's temperament and thinking. They themselves go to extra lengths to play down their Muslim identity and instead flaunt their lack of religiosity while arguing against burqas, skullcaps and mullahs. Their aggressive liberalism, however, puts off even moderate Muslims.

WHO ARE THEY?

It is a small, English-speaking urban elite of mostly left-wing non-practising Muslims including many atheists and agnostics who have about as much to do with Islam or the Muslim community as socialites with socialism. And I should know, because I am one of them. They, or rather we, are not only largely detached from the mainstream community but our approach to it is one of condescension, sometimes even bordering on contempt. The community, in turn, has no love lost for us and looks upon us with suspicion. We are seen as outsiders and untrustworthy. Devout Muslims find our views on Islamic issues annoying and patronizing. Let alone mullahs, even moderates are put off by our secularism which is at times almost militant, and often confrontational in approach.

As Faizur Rahman, an independent Islamic researcher and founder of Chennai-based Islamic Forum For the Promotion of Modern Thought, told me:

> The problem with most atheistic liberals is that they wear their atheism on their sleeves and are as preachy as sectarian clerics. Also, the believers are put off by the display of excessive left-wing rationalism which is projected as the only cure for all ills facing a religious community. I know of Muslim 'liberals' who think that Muslims would progress

only when they start questioning the authorship of their holy book, the Quran. These overenthusiastic 'reformers' rely on the outdated views of medieval commentators to conclude that "the Quran is far from the human rights or gender equality document that Muslim apologists make it out to be." This is akin to Islamophobes asserting the correctness of the ISIS understanding of Islam to demonize Muslims. Certainly, the Muslim community will not take them seriously.

There is a term commonly used to describe left-wing liberals like us: *naam ke mussalman* (Muslims only in name.) My friends jokingly used to call me a 'G&T Mussalman' for my gin-and-tonic lunch routine. And I am not the only G&T Muslim. There are other more high-profile Muslims whose brand of liberalism (dismissive of religion and the idea of religious identity; rubbishing Islamic precepts; abandoning Muslim Personal Law in favour of secular laws, etc.) strikes all the wrong notes for a conservative community. They exist in a parallel universe where notions of faith and religious identity are not quite the same as those of mainstream Muslims.

FAUX CONSCIENCE-KEEPERS

So far, not so bad. Just some liberals caught up in a comedy of errors. The problem arises when they try to assume the role of the moral conscience and guide of millions of Indian Muslims while lacking any empathy for them and without making any attempt even to listen to them, or have a dialogue with them. They have been likened to a latter-day version of white missionaries who took it upon themselves to 'civilize' the natives. Except that those missionaries made an effort to reach out to the people they wished to influence—learning their language, and going and living among them to win their hearts and minds. A far cry from the patronizing approach of our Left liberal Muslim saviours. Indeed, if I were a mainstream practising Muslim, I would be offended by their hectoring tone and tell them to shut up and go away.

Once, in my naïveté, I too saw myself in the role of a reformer pontificating from the secular pulpit of op-ed pages. It took me an awfully long time to realize that while my message might have been great, I was the wrong messenger. I didn't speak their language; they didn't understand mine. It was a dialogue of the deaf. I am reminded of a distant uncle, a well-read Urdu journalist and a minor writer. He was a chest-thumping atheist and enjoyed taking the mickey out of his religious Muslim friends, not sparing even his family members. He regarded the Muslim community as generally regressive and resistant to change. Yet, for all his obvious contempt for it, he felt entitled to assume that they would be all ears when he lectured them.

But why go back to a dead old uncle?

Take Javed Akhtar, one of the best known Muslim faces, extremely articulate, and regarded as a quintessential liberal Muslim, much in demand for his views on Muslim issues. But he is exactly the kind of liberal Muslim who gets on the nerves of even relatively moderate Muslims with his aggressive in-your-face liberalism dispensed from the high pedestal of atheism. A self-proclaimed proud atheist lecturing a deeply religious community on complex theological issues is a bit like a teetotaller trying to run a brewery. He has enraged Muslims, including moderates, by calling them bigots for objecting to being forced to chant 'Bharat Mata Ki Jai' by the RSS. Even Hindu liberals thought he had gone over the top when, in his farewell speech as a Rajya Sabha member on 15 March 2016, he insisted on chanting 'Bharat Mata Ki Jai" in the House as a riposte to Asaduddin Owaisi, leader of the right-wing All India Majlis-e-Ittehadul Muslimeen, who had said he would never chant the slogan because, 'Nowhere in the Constitution does it say that one should say Bharat Mata Ki Jai.'

Describing the scene, *Outlook* magazine (2 May, 2016) wrote:

Then very theatrically Akhtar displayed his uber-patriotism; he raised and dropped his right hand three times as he chanted *Bharat Mata ki Jai*, saying:

'I'm not interested in knowing whether it is my duty or not to say Bharat Mata ki jai,…it is my right. And I'm saying, *Bharat Mata ki Jai, Bharat Mata ki Jai, Bharat Mata ki Jai*'…. Akhtar then cynically noted that neither is there in the Constitution a requirement to wear sherwani and topi, Owaisi's regular attire. Shabana Azmi, Akhtar's wife, tried to be witty: 'Will Owaisi say "*Bharat Ammi Ki Jai*", if he has a problem saying *Bharat Mata Ki Jai*?'

WHO IS A LIBERAL MUSLIM?

As the writer of the above *Outlook* B.R. Gowani pointed out, this was not the first time Akhtar had tried to show off his patriotism as against the Muslim community's supposed bigotry.

> A couple of years ago, India lost the Asia Cup cricket match to Pakistan. A group of 67 Kashmiri students studying at Sharda University in Uttar Pradesh cheered the Pakistani team. They were suspended briefly. Akhtar emitted his patriotism...and tweeted: '*Why the suspension of those 67 Kashmiri students who cheered Pakistan is revoked? They should be rusticated and sent back to Kashmir.*'

Social media exploded with criticism of his remark. Responding to a tweet which said, 'Go get a life man. On (the) one hand u say Kashmir is integral part of India & on other hand you want to send them back. Shame,' Akhtar retorted: 'Shame on you that you are standing by those who were celebrating Indian team's defeat. They are traitors.'

Gowani described his reaction as 'dangerous nationalism coming from a writer who is a self-proclaimed secular, atheist, and liberal.'

Naseeruddin Shah, another uber liberal nominal Muslim, is a permanent source of annoyance to Muslims with his preachy interventions. He caused widespread outrage when apropos of nothing, he accused the community of being soft on Muslim extremists, wallowing in a sense of 'victimization' instead of taking responsibility for their condition, and being 'indifferent' to education and hygiene. What infuriated Muslims even more was that he went to extra lengths to disown his Muslim identity declaring that he was 'not a practising Muslim, and in fact had never been overly aware of a Muslim identity.'

In an article in *Hindustan Times* in June 2017, he was at pains to disown his 'Muslimness,' writing:

'My wife Ratna (Pathak) is Hindu, and we were married much before the term "love jihad" was coined and acted upon. She and I both have no more than a ritualistic connection with our respective religions.'

Criticizing Muslim attitudes, he said:

> It seems essential for Muslims in India to get over the feeling of victimization they are in now...we must determine to stop feeling persecuted, all evidence to the contrary notwithstanding; we must stop hoping for salvation from somewhere and take matters into our own hands—not least of all to take pride in our Indian-ness and assert our claim on our country. Indian Muslims' indifference, particularly among the economically weaker sections, to education or hygiene need not be reiterated, nor the fact that they have no one but themselves to blame for these ills. Granted, patriotism is not a tonic that can be forced down peoples' throats. But till the length of Sania Mirza's skirt causes more agitation than the lack of modern education and employment opportunities for our community, as long as we hesitate to condemn the sadistic madness of the ISIS (that we haven't heard too many Hindu voices condemn the lynching of innocent Muslims by gaurakshaks is immaterial), so long as we

continue to spawn 'believers' without giving a thought to their upbringing, or continue to dilly-dally on the removal of an outdated heavily misogynistic tradition, we only help reinforce the belief so easily held that we support or at least condone violence and regression.

His gratuitous comments were seen as not only insulting and patronizing but blatantly unfair—and likened to kicking someone when he is already down.

All lovely examples of bigotry spewed out daily to those the State either ignores, or oppresses, saying, 'you have none to blame but yourself. It is also a really insulting article that heaps contempt on the underprivileged, no matter how long ago he would have written it, it is contemptible. There is a significant difference between saying part of the problem has been an abysmal leadership among Indian Muslims, and saying that is the only problem, ignoring a political movement based on bigotry, violence and murder is governing the country and sets the agenda,

—Omair T Ahmad, writer and blogger.

One liberal Muslim social reformer who was widely hailed in the 1970s and 1980s was Hamid Dalwai, a Marathi activist of Jai Prakash Narayan's Indian Socialist Party, who left politics to concentrate on social reforms among Muslims. He has often been compared to great social reformers like B.R. Ambedkar and Jyotiba Phule, and is cited as a model liberal Muslim. Ramchandra Guha has singled him out as among a handful of post-independence Muslim leaders who 'had the potential to take their community out of a medievalist ghetto into a full engagement with the modern world.' (*The Indian Express*, 24 March, 2018)

The fact is that Dalwai himself was an extremist—a liberal fundamentalist, if you like—and his uncompromising and high pitched campaign stand on issues like the Muslim Personal Law which he wanted replaced by a Uniform Civil Code, ended up alienating many moderate Muslims who supported him initially. He was instead embraced by Maharashtra's Hindu right which, as noted academic Suhas Palshikar pointed out, used him 'to prove how Islam is flawed.' Palshikar wrote:

> He had far too many Hindu followers, more so posthumously, when sections of Hindutva politicians from Maharashtra began upholding him. Around the '90s, Dalwai was the most favoured for Savarkarite Hinduists in the state who quoted him to prove how Islam is flawed. The misappropriation of Dalwai was due to his trenchant critique of Islam....While intellectually, the rationalist critique of religion might be attractive, in a world of believers, to argue for change on the ground that religion has no sanctity in the lives of people is a sure way of alienating people from the reform agenda.
> (*The Indian Express*, 24 March, 2018)

Dalwai, who died young, was typical of liberal Muslims whose hardline liberalism is guaranteed to fail in a society marked by such a strong sense of faith identity irrespective of religion.

WHO IS A LIBERAL MUSLIM?

What Indian Muslims don't want is a Mustafa Kemal Ataturk-like figure who, rather than reforming and modernizing Islam, ended up de-Islamizing Turkey, with any hint of its display in public effectively banned, down to even wearing the traditional Fez cap. It may appear far-fetched but the Turks insist that it is a lingering backlash against Ataturk's delegitimization of Islam that is behind the creeping Islamization of Turkey under the current president, Recep Tayyip Erdogan. Iran, where Muslim zealots overthrew Reza Shah Pahlavi's modernizing regime to impose Islamic rule in 1979, is another example of the hazards of aggressive secularism in a conservative and religious society.

The Indian Muslim reaction has not been dissimilar. There are many reasons cited for the community's entrenched conservatism—lack of education, insecurity, 'minority psyche,' and perceived threat to Muslim identity from the Hindu Right. But what is not often mentioned is that it is also a reaction to attempts to impose a purist and absolutist idea of liberalism onto it. So, anyone who doesn't tick all the right boxes is cast as 'illiberal.' To qualify as a liberal, they must completely reject Sharia, unconditionally accept a secular uniform civil code, and shun any sense of religious identity. Anyone with a beard or in a burqa is *ipso facto* a 'fundo.' It is this Western Enlightenment template of an 'ideal' liberal that has made ordinary Muslims suspicious of hoity-toity left-wing liberal Muslims. They are as much responsible for creating a Muslim stereotype—mad mullahs, raving fanatics, oppressed women—as right-wing Hindu nationalists. What their sledgehammer approach—advocating a root-and-branch reform of Muslim practices—has done, is to unwittingly help the fundamentalists consolidate their grip on the community by raising the spectre of 'Islam in danger.' To a conservative Muslim in Jama Masjid, a JNU liberal demanding replacement of Muslim Personal Law with a uniform civil code, or shutting down madrassas, sounds more like a Hindu right-wing zealot than a Muslim well-wisher.

Amir Ali, who teaches at Jawaharlal Nehru University, says:

> The fundamental problem with the very idea of a liberal Muslim is that s/he would very likely be a 'good Muslim' rather than a 'bad Muslim' in the eyes of liberal establishments, if one were to use the binary offered by political scientist Mahmood Mamdani (Bombay-born Ugandan academic and commentator.) In other words, the liberal Muslim would likely be a figure saying precisely what liberal establishments want. It would almost seem as if liberal establishments have created a template for a good liberal-Muslim.

He objects to the hyphenated term 'liberal-Muslim' itself, arguing:

> ...the problem with hyphenated terms in which the liberal precedes the hyphen is that it tends to hegemonize, dominate and sometimes even eviscerate the possible potential of the term that comes after the hyphen. A serious case could then be made that the liberal component of the term liberal-Muslim is meant to dilute and thereby contain the Muslim part, making it that much more suspicious in the eyes of many Muslims.

WHO IS A LIBERAL MUSLIM?

Sometimes, it helps to play the Devil's Advocate in order to get a perspective on a complex issue. So, let me say this: notwithstanding the negative stereotype of a community drenched in extremism from head to toe, the reality is that most Muslims are moderate. The opposite of progressive is not fundamentalist. All Muslims may not be Oxford English Dictionary-compliant liberals, but that doesn't mean they are raving fundamentalists either.

The liberal tendency to look down upon every namaazi as illiberal, is naturally resented by Muslims, who say that such an attitude itself is a sign of illiberalism. If a church-going Christian and a temple-going Hindu can be liberal, they ask, is it so hard to accept that a mosque-going Muslim can also be liberal? Ok, not *liberal* liberal, but relatively liberal—who takes a moderate position on social issues and is open to persuasion and reform. There is also an assumption that barring an 'enlightened' urban elite, the Muslim community is overwhelmingly anti-reforms. It is again a perception problem to which, admittedly, Muslims themselves have contributed a great deal by attempting to defend—in the name of Muslim unity—what they know is indefensible.

The reality is that except for the mullahs, whose size and influence are often exaggerated, most mainstream Muslims acknowledge the need for reform. They may not be dying to embrace a uniform civil code, but there are specific areas, particularly relating to marriage and inheritance laws, which they believe need a fresh look. Here, the example of the Muslim woman cited earlier in this chapter, who takes a liberal position on triple talaq but insists on her daughter wearing hijab, is relevant. She may not qualify as a gold standard liberal, but she is clearly a moderate in relation to those who defend triple talaq. And she is not alone, but is part of a silent majority of moderate Muslims who find themselves caught between extreme liberals and extreme fundamentalists.

Meet Mohammed Aslam, a young car mechanic. He is a five-time namaazi and regards Sharia as an integral part of Islam but he says he is opposed to following it 'blindly.' There are provisions of Sharia he doesn't feel comfortable about. Punishment for blasphemy is one of them. 'Of course I don't want anyone to speak disrespectfully about Prophet Mohammad and might even pick up a fight if someone does it, but I don't want people to be sent to jail or killed for it. The Prophet himself would not have approved of it. But I can't say it openly because someone will get a fatwa against me and it will then be used to smear the whole community.'

Yet, people like Aslam seldom figure in the debate, and the popular narrative is of a community swarming with rigid status quoists. Probably, one reason for this perception is the community's strident opposition, cutting across the moderate-fundamentalist divide, to any perceived attempt by 'outsiders' to impose change. The legislation outlawing triple talaq is a case in point. Many moderate Muslims, though otherwise opposed to the practice, saw the move as an interference in their internal affairs, and the first step in a slippery slope to obliterating their

Muslim identity.

Ultimately, it boils down to that old chestnut: a lack of forward-looking leadership with a will and ability to create a favourable atmosphere for reforms. As things stand, the community has been hijacked by an unlikely alliance of unreconstructed fundamentalists and Left liberal Muslims, with both feeding on each other. Between them, they have created two extreme binaries: nothing short of full-blown Sharia (mullahs) versus nothing short of full-blown secularism (secular messiahs), squeezing out moderate views.

But there is a glimmer of hope in the form of a new crop of reform-minded Muslim youth who are quietly working to change attitudes. Many come from conservative backgrounds, are practising Muslims and very conscious of their identity, often sporting beards or hijab, but at the same time they are also modern, open-minded and secular. I wrote about them at length in my earlier book, *India's Muslim Spring: Why Is Nobody Talking About It?*

They have no pretensions of being liberals or nurse fantasies about secularizing the community overnight. Some themselves are suspicious of in-your-face secularism—and secularists. They don't have a manifesto or a grand strategy. They simply talk to fellow Muslims—friends, relations, neighbours—in a bid to start a dialogue around issues that they believe are holding back the community. Coming as they do from the same milieu, they enjoy their trust and carry a level of credibility that outsiders don't. My contention is that it is these home-grown moderate

Muslims—not 'imported liberals'—who will drive the change. For the simple reason that they *know* their community, empathize with it, and recognize how far it is prepared to go. They are aware of the limits of the community's appetite for reforms. More importantly, the community sees them as their 'own' (as against liberal messiahs come to save them) and is, therefore, more willing to listen to them.

Many of the Muslim women activists behind the successful campaign against triple talaq came from this cohort of young Muslims. It is important to point out that these women are not against ripping up the Muslim Personal Law altogether. In other words, in common with other moderates of their generation, they prefer a gradualist approach to reform, which has a better chance of succeeding in a conservative milieu than the Left liberals' quest for a total revolution overnight. Historically, in Islam, attempts to fast-track or force reforms have backfired and set the clock back—an issue I have dealt with later in this book. One reason why moderates lost out to the conservatives quite early in the history of Islam is because, among other things, they misjudged the prevailing mood and were often in a hurry to push reforms.

But let us cut to the chase. After flapping around for 70 years chasing the chimera of secular Islam, the time has finally come for champagne liberals to admit that we got it wrong. We got it wrong on messaging; we got it wrong on delivering the message; and most fundamentally and fatally, we got it wrong on the nature of post-independence Indian Muslim society—why, rightly or wrongly, it so desperately feels the need to be protective of its Muslimness. And we got all this wrong because we never really cared to engage with ordinary Muslims.

Lenin famously said he hated bourgeois liberals because they looked upon revolution as a 'finishing school.'

It is not a finishing school. Revolution is a messy business, he said. And so is trying to sell reforms to a socially conservative, religious and insecure community. For starters, it requires winning its trust. Which means venturing out of the cosy seminar circuit and Lutyens' bubble, and connecting with real Muslims—mixing with them, talking to them as equals, not patronizing them. There is still no guarantee of success but we will have at least tried.

If we find all this too messy, the honourable course, having so spectacularly bungled it, is for us to shut up and leave the job of reforming Indian Islam to those who are better placed to do it—the moderates within the community. Instead of dismissing them as 'soft' fundamentalists, we should support them in the very difficult task they are trying to do in a challenging environment.

India has a long history of liberal Muslim reformers who were also deeply religious (the sort our left-liberal set would have turned their noses at) and often used religion to sell their reforms—Sir Syed Ahmed, Zakir Husain and Abul Kalam Azad, just to mention a few household names.) Today's potential reformers may not be high-profile figures but this is not the age of big transformative figures anyway. It is the age of grassroots networks and collective initiatives—and sometimes they can be more effective than individual efforts. Armchair liberals can make themselves useful by supporting these campaigns. I, for one, am going to put my money where my mouth is—and shut up.

3

'OLD' LIBERALS VS 'NEW' LIBERALS

It used to be jokingly said about Indian Muslims that they were divided between two Ms: they were either mullahs or Marxists. It was, of course, a stereotype of a community which despite its monochromatic image has always been as diverse as any other religious group. But, to be sure, there was also an element of truth in the metaphorical mullah-Marx narrative. That was *the* Big Divide: mainstream conservatism versus a smattering of Left liberalism. There was nothing in-between—no middle ground. If there was, it was absent from public discourse. The public debate was only between the likes of Shahi Imam of Delhi's Jama Masjid and the likes of Shabana Azmi.

That Big Divide is no more. While conservatives remain very much in charge and continue to set the agenda, the Marxists have taken a battering. No, not at the hands of mullahs, but from a new class of in-house faith-bearing liberals who see themselves as true standard-bearers of liberal Islam, and consider faithless Marxist Muslims as pretenders. Their emergence marks a significant phase in the community's search for moderate liberal leadership. For the first time, we have a class of middle-of-the-road liberals who don't see faith and liberalism in terms of an either/or binary. Unlike Left liberal Muslims, they believe that you can be both a believer—a devout practising Muslim—*and* a liberal.

But it has also opened up a new divide in the community: moderate liberal Muslims versus hardline liberal Muslims, the so-called Marxist liberals. It is still early days but the new liberal kid on the block is already on a warpath against Old Guard liberals. And their hostility feeds into the mainstream Muslims' pent-up frustration with Left liberals who they call 'sarkari Muslims.'

The following episode offers a rare glimpse into the simmering *liberal versus liberal* war. It is also significant because it flips the myth of a united, monolithic community and shows us a people engaged in furious argument among themselves. Hence, I am presenting it at length.

In December 2018, Naseeruddin Shah, an outspoken critic of both Muslim and Hindu conservatives, gave an interview to a rights group, Karwan-e-Mohabbat India, in which he spoke of heightened insecurity among minorities, and said intolerance had grown so much that he worried for his children.

'I feel anxious for my children because tomorrow if a mob surrounds them and asks: "Are you a Hindu or a Muslim?" they will have no answer. Because they have no religion... We chose to not give any religious education to our children,' he said, while alluding to killings of several Muslims by cow vigilantes on suspicion of eating or selling beef. He emphasized that his wife Ratna Pathak Shah was not Muslim.

He also referred to the death of a police officer, Subodh Kumar Singh, in mob violence in Bulandshahr, western Uttar Pradesh, following rumours of cow slaughter, and said:

> There is complete impunity for those who take law into their own hands. In many areas we are witnessing that the death of a cow is more significance than that of a police officer.'
> (Bangalore Mirror, 20 Dec, 2018)

Now, Shah is used to being bullied by both Hindu and Muslim bigots depending on who he has offended at a given point in time. So he was not ruffled when right-wing Hindu nationalists got on his case, declaring him anti-national, telling him to go to Pakistan, offering him a one-way ticket to Karachi, etc. He shrugged off the attacks saying he wasn't surprised.

What he had not expected and what took him by complete surprise was the backlash from fellow liberal Muslims who, he had assumed, were his allies in fighting intolerance and communalism. A classic case of *'Et tu Brutus?'* Suddenly, Shah was at the centre of a simmering culture war in which he found himself cast as a 'pseudo liberal' by moderate practising Muslims. (Remember BJP leader L.K. Advani's famous 'pseudo secular' jibe at Congress secularists?) They took to Twitter and the blogosphere to denounce him, describing him as part of a privileged Muslim elite which spoke up only when it felt threatened, while conveniently choosing to remain silent when ordinary Muslims were under attack.

> He's suddenly found his tongue. Great. Who does he find it for, 'Oh, even people like us may be in danger.' At a time when innocents have been murdered regularly, such a late, narrow realization, is not something to be lauded. I spit on the fears of the privileged that open their mouths only when the monster arrives at their door, stained with the blood and misery of the poor and vulnerable for whom they have said nothing.
>
> (Tweeted by Omar T. Ahmad, a writer and researcher)

Another wrote:

'As for Shah's comments on feeling his children aren't safe. Come on, they're very privileged, unlike the family of Pehlu Khan (a dairy farmer killed by cow vigilantes with alleged links to right-wing Hindutva groups.) For the former, prejudice is inconvenient. For the latter, it is death.'

Many were particularly angered by his attempt to distance himself from his Muslim identity by repeatedly underlining that he was not a practising Muslim and nor had he brought up his children to be religious. Irena Akbar, an entrepreneur and a practising self-proclaimed Muslim, wrote that non-practising liberal Muslims like Shah were 'pseudo liberals' and hypocrites. She accused them of 'publicly mocking ordinary Muslims.' She was apparently trolled for her comments, upon which she wrote: 'From the way I have been mobbed for my tweet on pseudo-liberal Muslims, I have learnt one thing: As an ordinary practising Muslim, you cannot, must not, dare not question the public political utterings of self-proclaimed non-practising Muslims.' A young lawyer said: 'He's effectively telling the lynch mobs: leave me alone, I've nothing to do with Muslims.'

Such a public display of divisions is unprecedented for a community that likes to keep its differences to itself and present a united face to the outside world. It can be interpreted either as a sign that the rift has got too big for it to hide; or, as many Muslims believe, an indication of a new confidence among Muslims that allows them to air their differences openly.

According to Dr Uzma Azhar who teaches at Jamia Millia Islamia, Delhi, the community is going through a big churning process and the new openness is a part of this process. As a student of identity politics and a young practising liberal Muslim herself, she says she is 'fascinated' by the debate. What particularly fascinates her is how the Muslim caste and class divide (mostly invisible to the outside world) is playing out in the liberalism row. Theoretically, Islam doesn't recognize caste and takes pride in being the most egalitarian religion, but Indian Muslims have taken the idea of *'Ganga-Jamni tehzeeb'* to an extreme and have developed an elaborate caste hierarchy defined by lineage and family profession. Broadly, it is split between Ashrafs (Muslim equivalents of Brahmins) and the non-Ashrafs known as Ajlaf. Not quite as oppressive as the Hindu caste system, but we are getting there.

Most Left liberals happen to come from upper classes (so-called Ashrafs.) Which makes them look more elitist and different from ordinary Muslims they presume to represent. A fact their moderate liberal rivals have been quick to seize upon, to question their supposed concern for the community.

In 2015, Bollywood actor/filmmaker Amir Khan, speaking at an event in New Delhi, said that minorities in India were feeling increasingly insecure after a series of attacks and even he and his wife had discussed leaving the country out of concern for their child.

> When I chat with Kiran at home, she says, Should we move out of India?' That is a disastrous and big statement for Kiran to make. She fears for her child. She fears about what the atmosphere around us will be. She feels scared to open the newspapers every day.
>
> (While speaking at the Ramnath Goenka Excellence in Journalism Awards, in Delhi, on 22 Nov, 2015)

Amir was roundly attacked by Bharatiya Janata Party (BJP), branded an anti-national and told to go to Pakistan if he was not happy in India. Ironically, a lot of Muslims were not amused either by his intervention. Not because they disagreed with what he said but because of "who" he was—a privileged celebrity Muslim presuming to speak for a community he barely knew, according to his critics. Asaduddin Owaisi, head of the All India Majlis-e-Ittehadul Muslimeen, accused him of talking 'nonsense.' He thought Khan had played into the right-wing Hindu nationalists' narrative about Muslims not being nationalistic enough.

'I would have never said what Aamir said. We have seen numerous riots but still we continue to live here as it is our country,' he said. (*Huffington Post*, 24 Nov, 2015) He suggested that Muslims like Khan lived in a bubble.

Some other Muslims accused him of grandstanding.

'A lot of us felt that he was showing off. What does he know about insecurities? He was only concerned about his child. And his solution was to pick his bags and leave India,' a friend, who didn't want to go on record, told me.

Generally, however, Muslims refrained from airing their criticism publicly for fear of appearing to give legitimacy to the Hindu Right's attacks on Khan. Since then, however, they are said to have become less wary and more relaxed about discussing intra-community issues in public. It is claimed that this is a sign of a new confidence driven by younger Muslims who are not afraid to ask hard questions without looking over their shoulders. While it is true that the young are more confident and open-minded, there is no evidence of this permeating through the rest of the community. If anything, the dominant mood is one of despondency, insecurity and resignation.

At this point the obvious question to ask is: Where is the so-called churning headed? Is it the starting guns for a more liberal Indian Islam?

To be candid, I am slightly sceptical about the churning itself. Yes, some people are talking among themselves and exchanging views, which is refreshing, but it is more of a chatter—and mostly confined to online chat rooms and social media sites. It does not even constitute a proper debate. Calling it churning, which implies a process of fundamental change, is an exaggeration. It is striking how little discussion there is on reforms; on the other hand, there is disproportionate focus on identity-related issues and a strong pushback against any dissenting viewpoint.

In the course of writing this book, I attended a number of seminars held under the aegis of various Muslim groups in universities and elsewhere, ostensibly to discuss reforms. Speakers at these meetings included Muslim intellectuals, political figures, students and activists. I saw these gatherings as a good opportunity to pick up the educated and moderate Muslim viewpoint on the challenges the community faces, and in particular, their take on the pressing need for social and religious reform. I went to these events precisely because they were billed as discussions on the way forward for Indian Muslims. However, almost each one of them turned into a platform for cataloguing Muslim grievances; a litany of stories of victimhood—with no mention of reforms or any hint of introspection. One well-known academic who was on the panel of speakers at one of the seminars was booed and called 'anti-Muslim' when he questioned the Muslim 'fixation' with identity and a lack of will to reform.

It was a dispiriting experience; enough to disabuse me of any notion that a liberal Muslim awakening is imminent. Or that it is even an aspiration for the majority of the community or those who presume to speak for it. To be sure, there are individual liberal voices—small groups like the Chennai-based Islamic Forum for the Promotion of Moderate Thought and Mumbai-based Bharatiya Muslim Mahila Andolan who are quietly working for change—but one swallow does not make a spring.

So, to cadge a phrase from Lenin: Where do we go from here? My money is still on the middle-of-the-road *namaazi-parhezgar*, the devout moderates whose cautious and gradualist approach is likely to win more converts than the wilder fantasies of Left liberals. Hopefully, in time to come they will shed some of their obsession with the idea of an immutable and fixed Muslim identity, and learn to be less prickly about criticism (No, Ramchandra Guha is not an Islamophobe.) The cause of moderation is not served by defensive knee-jerk reactions. They also need to be careful to avoid taking positions that could allow the fundamentalists to ride piggyback and push their own line. In their visceral hostility towards doctrinaire Left liberals, moderates often veer into positions that are promptly seized by doctrinaire conservatives to claim 'we-told-you-so.'

There must be no confusion that between the two doctrinaire tendencies—the comrades and the mullahs—which one poses the greater threat: the mullahs, of course. The clash of liberals must not obscure this reality.

To conclude on an optimistic note, in the words of Faiz Ahmed Faiz:

> *Aayei haath uthaen hum bhī*
> *hum jinheñ rasm-e-duā yaad nahīñ*
> *hum jinheñ soz-e-mohabbat ke sivā*
> *koī but ka.ī khudā yaad nahīñ.*

(Come let us also raise hands for prayers; we who do not even remember the rituals of prayers.)

4

LIBERAL ROOTS OF INDIAN ISLAM

Long before 'alternative facts' and fake news gained currency, right-wing Hindu nationalists were already peddling an alternative history of Indian Islam, distorting well-documented facts about its origins and presenting it as a malign and illiberal influence on ethnic Indian culture. In that narrative, Muslims came to India as invaders and today's Indian Muslims are *Babur ki Aulad* (descendants of Babur) who must collectively pay for his sins. This 'alternative' version of history also invokes visions of successive Muslim rulers as cultural vandals with a mission to Islamize Hindu culture.

No sensible debate on Indian Muslims or Islam is possible

unless we first clear the fog of fake history that is fast creeping into mainstream scholarship with textbooks being rewritten to formalize it. So, let us first get our history right: how Islam arrived in India and developed—assimilating, as much as influencing, the local cultural landscape as it spread gradually across the country.

BEFORE THE ADVENT OF THE MUGHALS

The historical fact is that Babur, who founded the Mughal Empire in India and whose name and actions are routinely invoked to damn Indian Muslims, came to India nearly 800 years after Islam had already set down roots here and assumed a distinctively multicultural character by assimilating local cultural practices. The Mughal Empire was established in 1526 with Babur's accession to the throne, and lasted more than 300 years—ending with the defeat of Bahadur Shah Zafar at the hands of the British in 1857, though its decline had started right after the death of Aurangzeb in 1707. But, to come back to the origins of Indian Islam, the first Muslims came to India as early as the seventh century CE—and they came as traders, NOT as invaders. The maiden ship carrying Arab traders landed on the western coast of Malabar and Konkan; and what is thought to be India's first mosque, was built in Kerala in 629 CE. Called the Cheraman Juma Masjid and located in Thrissur, it was built by Malik Deenar, a Persian ex-slave and a companion of the Prophet, on the orders of Cheraman Perumal, the Chera King of the region who had converted to Islam. Non-Muslims also use it for certain initiation rituals, even now.

LIBERAL ROOTS OF INDIAN ISLAM

The Islam that emerged in India as a result of its interaction with local cultural practices and rituals was more moderate than elsewhere—a product of a syncretic culture popularly referred to as *Ganga-Jamni tehzeeb* in which Hindus and Muslims participated in each other's festivals—even adopted practices from each other and made them their own. The Mughals, for instance, celebrated Holi in a big way. Even Babur was said to be 'so wonderstruck' by Holi celebrations, according to Urdu historian Zakaullah, that he 'filled a pool with his favourite coloured liquid—wine.' (Khalid Alvi, an Urdu academic, *The Indian Express*, 8 April, 2019) Today, however, many Indian Muslims regard playing Holi as un-Islamic.

Muslim rulers, both during the Delhi Sultanate (1206-1526) and the Mughal era, followed a policy of non-interference in religious practices. They made efforts to avoid offending non-Muslim sensitivities with stress on religious and cultural co-existence. Akbar not only banned cow slaughter but discouraged meat eating generally in a nod to Hindu sensitivities on the issue.

According to Dr Uzma Azhar of Jamia Millia Islamia, Indian securliasm can be traced back to the Akbar era. He believed in pluralism in matters of faith and offered State protection to minorities.

Akbar wrote: 'The multitude should practice *Sulh-i kul*— mutual and peaceful understanding, with the world and with all humankind… Everyone who comes to the path of reason is fortunate. And everyone who remains miserable in the barren land of tradition is an invalid. Every person who recognizes and worships God in whatever way is welcome, (http://www.openthemagazine.com/article/lost-found-histories/the-akbari-synthesis-and-india-s-plurality)

Dara Shikoh, whose rivalry with brother Aurangzeb resulted in his death, also had a reputation as a scholar and humanist prince who was interested in understanding the religious philosophy of other faiths. He translated the Upanishads and believed in co-existence with other religions. Often the struggle for the throne is also depicted as the struggle between the liberal values of Dara Shikoh and Aurangzeb's strict adherence to the Sharia principles. Although it would be very simplistic to see them through the prism of religion, it was one of the factors that dominated the politics of that era.

A key moderating influence on Indian Islam was Sufism. It had a profound impact on the acceptance and popularity of Islam in India. It owes its massive spread to Sufi preachers who travelled the length and breadth of the country to propagate it. They reached out to the poor and marginalized communities in rural areas and preached in local dialects. Their devotional practices and stress on piety and inclusion attracted people from all faiths and strata of society. By the thirteenth century, Sufism had become a formidable nationwide movement, eventually emerging as a major moral and philosophical force influencing all religious traditions including Hinduism. Despite the rise of

Wahhabism, which is opposed to any form of mysticism, Sufism became and remains a large part of Indian Islam.

RISE OF CONSERVATIVE ISLAM

The conservative strain in Indian Islam which had been kept under control by Muslim rulers, really manifested itself after the British came and the community suddenly found itself stripped of its special status. Muslims, who had previously formed the ruling class, saw themselves in danger of losing power and they responded to it by seeking refuge behind their religious identity which then became the focus of their anti-colonial political campaign. They feared that after the British left India, Muslim identity would no longer be safe in a Hindu-majority country. This was the trigger for Islamic revivalism, leading to the emergence of myriad movements from early nineteenth century onwards—the Mujahidins, the Faraizis, Deoband School, the Ahl-e-Hadiths, Aligarh School, Nadwat-ul-ulema, the Tablighi Jamaat and Jamaat-e-Islami, and Muslim modernists.

There was also a subtle shift away from the more liberal practices—from 'religiousness to religious-mindedness,' as Deoband came to represent the traditionalists, and Aligarh represented the Modernists.' (*Islam and Muslim History in South Asia, Francis Robinson, 2000*)

The Deoband School established in the year 1867 derived its tradition from the Indian Wahhabi movement of Shah Wali Ullah Dehlavi (1703-1762), scholar, theologian and philosopher. It is the most important theological academy of the Muslim world after Cairo's Al-Azhar. Mohammad Qasim Nanautawi (1833-77) and Rashid Ahmad Gangohi (1829-1905) developed Deoband as an institution. Maulvi Habibur Rahman, leading maulvi of Dar ul Uloom Deoband, was a journalist and a writer who also edited two Urdu monthlies, *Al Qasim* and *Al Rashid*.

Barbara Metcalf, in her book, *Islamic Revival in British India*, traces the Ulema response to colonial rule through the Deoband movement. First school was founded in 1867 and taught a reformed Islam, and owed nothing to the State. It was supported by public subscription, and was established as a modern bureaucratic organization. British historian Francis Robinson elaborates on how Deoband preached Islam. He says it created a form of Islam in which the State was irrelevant and in which any form of contact with Hindu religious practices were avoided. It concentrated on spreading Islamic knowledge as widely as possible. It envisaged no merging of its Islamic world with Indian national life or with institutions of modern State. The Deobandi strategy meant that the Ashraf (upper caste Muslims) believed that if they lived 'better Muslim lives' not only would they have fresh cultural and spiritual strength as individuals, but also the political fortunes of the community would be transformed, It was, as Metcalf points out, 'a very Gandhian vision of the road to independence.'

As Islam tried to rid itself of the 'corrupt' (read: syncretic/ borrowings from Hinduism) practices, it became more and more exclusivist. The best-known example of Hindu-Muslim syncretism is the influence of Bhakti movement on Sufism—an influence that endures even today. According to scholars like Rasheeduddin Khan and S.T. Lokhandwalla, the interaction between the Bhakti movement and Sufism exemplify the best of India's composite culture. 'One of the main factors of diversity in Islam is due to Sufism,' writes academic J.J. Roy Burman in his book *Hindu-Muslim Syncretic Shrines and Communities* which traces the roots of Hindu-Muslim syncretism. He attributes it to a number of factors, including trade, migration, missionary activities of mystics (sadhus and saints), inter-community and inter-faith marriages. And such efforts were encouraged by the State. Even Babur supported such efforts, and Akbar even launched an eclectic faith Din-e-Ilahi. Conservative Muslim reformers saw some of the practices that Muslims had borrowed from Hindus as un-Islamic. They were opposed to praying and worshipping at Sufi shrines and mazaars, likening it to a form of idolatory, which Islam opposes.

Reformers stressed the fundamentals of Islam—i.e. the points at which it differed from other faiths. The result was a more communalist Islam. Opposed to the Deoband School, the Bareilly (Barelvi) School emerged in U.P., led by Ahmad Raza Khan Barelvi (1856-1921.) It expressed and sustained the social and religious customs of what the reformist schools saw as a 'decadent' people. They adhered to the prevailing customs and superstitions, saint worship and other supposedly 'un-Islamic' practices. Their Islam was the actual religion followed in the villages of India.

The second strand was of Muslim Modernism under the

leadership of Sir Saiyyid Ahmad Khan (1817-98), the Aligarh movement and the Muslim League (1906.) Poet-philosopher Muhammad Allama Iqbal called Muslims in the name of Islam, exhorting them to be active, and not be idle or 'static.' He insisted boldly that a dynamic infidel is more righteous than a passive Muslim. In 1906, Muslim League was formed to seek political rights for Muslims and to protect them against Hindu domination. From the debris of the First World War, the Khilafat agitation (1920-22) and the subsequent bitter disillusionment, the Muslim bourgeoisie emerged emotionally both anti-British and anti-Hindu. Isolated and relatively weak.

Khilafat agitation had made the community more conscious of itself. One of the important elements in the new movement was its emphasis on Islam as a civilizing force. Leaders such as Mohammad Ali and Shaukat Ali reflected the changes in the dynamics of the community, as symbolism (clothes, etc.) became more prominent. In 1930, Iqbal put forth the idea of a Muslim State, which was adopted by the League in the 1940s. Jinnah in his 19 November, 1940 speech, quoted Gandhi in the Legislative Assembly, as referring to the Hindus and Muslims as 'we' and 'you.' It came against the background of Hindu Reform movements of the nineteenth century which had created a discourse in defence of 'our threatened religion,' according to which, Hindu society had to be defended against external weakness caused by conversions to 'foreign religions,' and differences and conflicts among Hindus themselves. The emphasis on oppression faced by the Hindus as 'subjects' under

LIBERAL ROOTS OF INDIAN ISLAM

the oppressive and barbaric Muslim and British rule, created differences between the two communities. Gandhi attempted to forge a compromise between the religious and secular wings of the Independence movement. Jinnah and the Muslim League regarded this as 'Hinduization of nationalist movement' and demanded a separate State for Muslims—ultimately leading to the creation of Pakistan in 1947.

It is interesting to note that for a religion which takes pride in its egalitarianism, class and caste play a big role in the lives of Indian Muslims. This I discuss elsewhere in the book. Historically, all Muslim reformist movements have turned on the class/caste divide—represented broadly by Ashrafs (literally meaning noble; they claim to be descendants of Prophet Mohammad), and Aijlas (lower classes comprising Hindu converts and/or engaged in menial professions.)

Commenting on the role of class, Francis Robinson writes,

> In the nineteenth century, effort was concentrated on a literate elite, the aristocracy, which was attracted to the *Ahl-i Hadiths* and *Ah-i Quran*; the *sharif* classes which tended to go to Aligarh and the lesser bourgeoisie of the *qasbas* which tended to go to Deoband; in the twentieth century... Jamaat-i Islami which though elitist itself, spoke to a whole new generation of Western-educated Muslims through Tablighi Jam'aat, or Preaching society, which aimed to, or aims to, involve ordinary Muslims in taking a basic understanding of reformist Islam to the masses. (*Islam and Muslim History in South Asia*, Francis Robinson)

61

The second half of the nineteenth century, however, saw leaders of the modernist movement of Aligarh, ulemas of Deoband and Firangi Mahal ulema, all come together in a show of Muslim unity cutting across social, cultural, and political divisions. Figures like Sir Saiyyid Ahmad Khan, Maudoodi, Iqbal emphasized the primacy of 'action.' Iqbal said in *Reconstruction of Religious Thought in Islam*, 'world is to be made and remade through continuous action' and on 'self reflection' over other considerations. It marked a significant shift from the 'other-wordly' to 'this-worldly,' emphasizing the urgent need for action *now* as against spiritual concerns. But the effort didn't really get too far as the Western-educated elites' emphasis on individualism contrasted with the communitarian ideals of Islam. And, essentially, we are still where we were then. Contrafactual historians reckon that things might have been different had Partition not intervened, leading to an exodus of the educated Muslim elite—leaving behind a mostly uneducated and culturally conservative lot wary of any change that might undermine their religious identity. Seventy years on, and despite the emergence of an educated and professional Muslim middle class, the community still remains intriguingly suspicious of far-reaching reforms. Muslim identity still trumps change.

5

HOW LIBERAL ISLAM LOST THE BATTLE

A word commonly mentioned in any discussion on Muslim extremism is hijack. There is a popular narrative which says that a historically tolerant religion has been 'suddenly' hijacked by extremists. But the reality is that liberal Islam lost out to extremists very early in its history and though it has had sporadic comebacks, notably under the Ottomans, it has mostly struggled in the face of challenges from its right-wing dissidents though the sort of violent extremism we are seeing now is new.

But there is nothing sudden about the phenomenon itself.

Ideologically, today's Wahhabis and jihadis come from a long line of an anti-liberal, anti-reform and intolerant strain in Islam that has sought to preserve it in its 'purest of pure' form as supposedly handed down by God. They are the spiritual heirs of the notorious Kharijites, a militant sect of dissenters in early Islam that believed in the most austere form of Islam and advocated violence against anyone who didn't accept their version. Fanatically monotheistic and intolerant, the Kharijites version of Islam emphasizes a strict adherence to a literalist reading of the Quran and Sunnah—teachings and practices of Prophet Mohammad—and advocated the killing of anyone who deviated from its understanding of Islam. Some scholars have described it as the first terrorist movement in Islamic history, and the so-called Islamic State fighters are often referred to as modern-day Kharijites.

What is important to note is that this extremist tendency emerged in the very first century of the founding of Islam and flourished during much of what is known as its 'golden age,' giving some idea of its influence. So, extremism in Islam goes all the way back to its inception and though it suffered a massive defeat after its initial surge, it never went away and has been popping up with frequent regularity under different signboards. There is nothing 'sudden' or unusual about Taliban, al-Qaeda or IS. At their core, they have the same DNA as the Kharijites. In its intolerance and fundamentalist beliefs, even the 1979 Islamic Revolution in Iran that brought Ayatollah Khomeini's hardline regime to power—and was hailed by India's liberal Left as a great anti-west imperialist moment—was actually a variant of the same extremist tendency.

Although Islam was founded on the noble principles of love, peace and brotherhood, the unfortunate fact is that it has had a bloody history. Three of its four Caliphs—Hazrat Umar, Hazrat Uthman and Hazrat Ali—were assassinated in a series of violent feuds after Prophet Mohammad's death. Ziauddin Sardar, noted British-Pakistani Islamic scholar, has written that Islam's history has been 'inherently violent.'

Claims to the contrary are based on a cherry-picked reading of Islam's chequered history—just as the extremists' defence of their actions are based on a selective interpretation of Quran and Hadith, the two main sources of Islamic theology. It ignores the arc of intolerance and repression that dogged Islam as rival schools of thought competed for supremacy and patronage of the ruler of the day. A tendency towards revisionism and to make the past look good by not allowing facts to come in the way of a good story, is not unique to Muslims (the idea of a Hindu 'golden age' is as much an exercise in revisionism) and the temptation becomes the greater when a culture or community feels it is being 'targeted.' Today, Muslims face relentless pressure to answer for the actions of their rogue co-religionists and their instinctive reaction is to defend Islam, glossing over the historical warts and presenting a prettified picture of its chequered past. Admittedly, there have been moments when I too have been sufficiently riled to react in a defensive way. So, I can see where the apologists are coming from: 'Islam is under attack, we must defend it.' But the problem arises when denial becomes the official narrative and is touted as the only truth in town.

And the problem is this: a vast majority of ordinary Muslims—like their Hindu, Christian and Sikh peers—are not exactly up to speed about their faith's history, and therefore are unable to challenge either the moderates' prettified version or the extremists' cherry-picked interpretation. So, whichever narrative they choose to accept, they end up with a skewed understanding of Islam. The result is a dangerously polarized global Muslim ummah.

Commenting on the gulf between British and American understanding of English, George Bernard Shaw apocryphally joked that Britons and Americans are two peoples divided by a common language. The same can be said about the contrasting narratives around Islam: the global Muslim ummah are two peoples divided by a common faith. Except that Americans and Brits still try and manage to communicate, whereas the two polarized Muslim groups are not even *trying* to communicate.

But the crisis facing moderate Islam is no joking matter; and what is often ignored is that this crisis precedes al-Qaeda and IS. And the crisis will only deepen if there is no acknowledgement that Islam has had an extremism problem through much of its history. The 'Islam-has-always-been-peaceful-and-consensual' narrative is problematic not only because it is historically not true, but because it generates complacency by suggesting that the current wave of extremism is simply an aberration which will pass, and in due course Islam will be restored to its old peaceful and consensual glory. Basically the message is: No need to do anything, just sit back, and it will pass.

That is why most Muslims appear simply bored by all the fuss; their concern is limited to extremist violence and acts of Islamist terror because it has personal consequences for them: every new terror attack in the name of Islam means another anti-Muslim backlash, more Islamophobia, more Muslim bans, and more negative perception of Muslims and Islam.

Whenever a Muslim hears of a terror attack, the first reaction is: 'Hope there is no Muslim behind it.' Their condemnation of violence committed by Muslims in the name of Islam is generally prompted by the fear of anti-Muslim reprisals as a result of such violence rather than a concern about the broader crisis of extremism in Islam. Take out the violence bit, and few Muslims are interested in addressing the central issue: the gradual erosion of moderate Islam and its regression into intolerance and parochialism. The fact, as I pointed out in the preceding chapter, that even liberal Muslims think they need to defend such obviously regressive 'symbols of Muslim identity' as burqa and skullcaps doesn't bode well for progressive Islam. Reclaiming black identity—Black is Beautiful—as a riposte to racism is one thing; reclaiming discarded symbols of patriarchy and oppression in response to Islamophobia, which itself is a reaction to Muslim extremism is quite another.

But, as British rights activist Sarah Khan writes:

> The battle within Islam, however, encompasses much more than just the challenge of terrorism. At its heart is a conflict

of ideas and a question as to whether Muslims believe Islam is reconcilable with pluralism and human rights.

(*The Battle for British Islam: Reclaiming Muslim Identity from Extremism*, Sarah Khan)

As I write, the world is cheering the defeat of IS just as it cheered the 'collapse' of al-Qaeda a few years ago. One, claims of a sweeping military victory are exaggerated as they were in the case of al-Qaeda as we saw subsequently. But even if the last IS/al-Qaeda/Boko Haram militant was killed, it would not magically usher in moderate Islam. Only violence will end; that too only until such time as the remnants of these groups are able to reorganize themselves and emerge under a new management.

In fact, nothing will change so long as millions of Muslims around the world continue to buy—as they do across the Middle East, Africa, Asia and Europe—into the extremists' interpretation of Islam, even if they condemn their violent methods.

The Wahhabi/Salafi Islam practised in Saudi Arabia—the self-appointed custodian of global ummah—which is exported abroad, is just another version of extremist Islam minus its violent strain; as is Iran's brand of Shia Islam. Between them, the two rival Muslim 'super powers' follow the most regressive versions of Sunni and Shia Islam respectively, and have invested heavily in propagating them. And these versions are closer to the extremists' version (minus the violence) than the tolerant and benign Islam of our ideals.

There is no point to keep denying that the extremists' version is 'not Islam' or a 'travesty' of Islam. It is as disingenuous as the claims that the lynch mobs going around India attacking suspected beef-eaters are 'not Hindus.' They may not represent the mainstream Islam but as I argue elsewhere in this book, they are very much in a long line of Islam's militant tendency. Their cherry-picking of obscure and ambiguous Islamic scriptures to justify their actions is no doubt opportunistic, but doesn't wholly negate the basis of their claims. Islamic scriptures are a minefield of ambiguity and a god-send for anyone wanting to exploit them for their own ends. While jihadis have been quick to do exactly that, the moderates' response has been slow, half-hearted, confused and patronizing, dismissing the Islamists as a bunch of thugs who have nothing to do with Islam and doomed to fail.

Thanks to this sort of complacency ('let us just wait it out and everything will be fine') there has been no reformist movement for almost a hundred years, while the fundamentalists have been expanding their influence. The destruction of the Ottoman Empire—the last and the greatest of Muslim military powers in the world—in the First World War, was a turning point in causing Islam's historic retreat from engagement with Western modernism. The Western colonization of the Muslim world was not only a military and political humiliation for Muslims but a body blow to their pride and psyche. They were blindsided by its impact, triggering a sense of demoralization so deep that they sought to escape it by seeking refuge in the past. Calls for a return to a pristine Islam became a battle-cry of conservatives who saw the Muslim plight as divine retribution for their having 'strayed' from the original tenets of Islam under Western influence. The appeal had widespread resonance among Muslims across the world and the idea of restoring Muslim 'honour' through jihad against its 'enemies' (the West), was on a roll.

Turkish scholar Mustafa Akyol has written how the switch from Ijtihad (reason) to jihad (struggle) occurred in an anti-West backlash in the late nineteenth and early twentieth centuries as the Muslim world was 'trampled' upon by Christian European powers.

> In just a few decades, nearly the whole Muslim world was attacked, invaded, and occupied by non-Muslim nations... These European countries, whose liberal values had impressed and inspired Islamic modernists, were now seen as trampling on the honour of Muslim nations, whose very borders were created arbitrarily by the new masters... The foreign invasions changed the entire intellectual landscape of Islamdom. The West was no longer a model to emulate but rather an intruder to eradicate. ...And the push for ijtihad would be overshadowed by the drive for jihad.
>
> (*Islam Without Extremes: A Muslim Case for Liberty,* Mustafa Akyol)

And that is where we still are more than a hundred years later, with no serious pushback from moderates. Meanwhile, we are in the absurd situation where some of the most fundamentalist countries—the original source of jihadism—have aligned with

Western powers to fight militant extremists while at the same time continuing to export and fund their own regressive brand of Islam across the world. So, even as IS fighters are being pummelled, another generation of jihadis is being bred with not a little ideological and material help from the same countries that are grandstanding over crushing the IS after it got too big for its boots. There is a self-perpetuating vicious cycle where the promoters of extremism find themselves scrambling to slay the monsters they themselves created, but who have now turned on them.

In a report in 2013, 'The Involvement of Salafism/Wahhabism in the Support and Supply of Arms to Rebel Groups Around the World,' commissioned by the Directorate-General for External Policies, the European Parliament noted that Wahhabi and Salafi groups mostly based in Saudi Arabia and other Gulf countries used Saudi charities to supply money and arms to rebel groups around the world.

Husain Haqqani, the former Pakistani ambassador to Washington and an expert on Muslim extremism, has accused Saudi Arabia's Wahhabi ideology (an offshoot of Salafism) of almost single-handedly destroying the pluralist tradition in Islam.

'The last few decades have seen this attempt to homogenize Islam' according to which 'there is only one legitimate path to God,' Haqqani was quoted as saying, by *New York Times* columnist Thomas L Friedman. And when there was only one legitimate path, Haqqani added, 'all others are open to being killed.' That has been the single most dangerous idea that has emerged in the Muslim world, and it came out of Saudi Arabia and has been embraced by others, including the government in Pakistan.'

That 15 of the 19 hijackers involved in the 9/11 atrocity came from Saudi Arabia is well-known, as is the fact that it has invested heavily in disseminating and actively promoting a brand of Islam that is a travesty of its central spirit.

> Nothing has been more corrosive to the stability and modernization of the Arab world, and the Muslim world at large, than the billions and billions of dollars the Saudis have invested since the 1970s into wiping out the pluralism of Islam—the Sufi, the versions—and imposing in its place the puritanical, anti-modern, anti-women, anti-Western, anti-pluralistic Wahhabi Salafist brand of Islam promoted by the Saudi religious establishment. It is not an accident that several thousand Saudis have joined the Islamic State or that Arab Gulf charities have sent ISIS donations. It is because all these Sunni jihadist groups—ISIS, Al Qaeda, the Nusra Front—are the ideological offsprings of the Wahhabism injected by Saudi Arabia into mosques and madrasas from Morocco to Pakistan to Indonesia.
>
> (Our Radical Islamic BFF, *Saudi Arabia New York Times*, 2 September, 2015)

A report in *The Times*, London, (16 July, 2014) claimed: 'For decades, Saudi Arabia has poured billions of its oil dollars into sympathetic Islamic organizations around the world, quietly practicing checkbook diplomacy to advance its agenda.' Documents published by WikiLeaks revealed how Riyadh sought not just to spread its strict version of Sunni Islam but also to undermine its pluralism.

The upshot is that no amount of breast-beating will help until the source of the toxic ideology that inspires jihadis is tackled. It is the ruling ideology of much of the Arab world and is spreading rapidly to other Muslim majority countries. Yet, we continue to pretend that extremists are not 'real' Muslims and don't represent 'real' Islam. It is intriguing that while Saudi Arabia and other countries that officially practise Wahhabi/ Salafi Islam are hailed as gold standard Muslims representing 'real Islam,' the jihadis who follow the same creed, albeit fuelled by some very brutal violence, are deemed heretics. Incidentally, some of the methods used by the ruling Islamic elites of Saudi Arabia, Iran and Pakistan are no less brutal. Like it or not, the Wahhabi/Salafi ruling elites and the gun-toting Salafi extremists are two sides of the same coin. If anything, the former are more dangerous because they are more powerful, wield more influence, and have more resources to propagate and enforce their intolerant ideology.

Indeed, we have had it straight from the horse's mouth. Saudi Crown Prince Mohammed bin Salman has admitted that his country got it wrong on Islam and promised to restore moderate Islam, describing it as key to his plans to modernize the kingdom. In a series of public speeches and media interviews since assuming power in 2017, he has sounded almost embarrassed over his country's hardline Islamic ideology. Saudi Arabia, he claimed, 'was not like this before 1979' alluding to the Islamic revolution in Iran and the occupation of Mecca's Grand Mosque by militants—suggesting that Wahhabism was a reaction to those events.

> What happened in the last 30 years is not Saudi Arabia. What happened in the region in the last 30 years is not the Middle East. After the Iranian revolution in 1979, people wanted to copy this model in different countries—one of them is Saudi Arabia. We didn't know how to deal with it. And the problem spread all over the world. Now is the time to get rid of it… We are simply reverting to what we followed—a moderate Islam open to the world and all religions. 70% of the Saudis are younger than 30, honestly we won't waste 30 years of our life combating extremist thoughts; we will destroy them now and immediately.
>
> (*The Guardian*, 24 October, 2017)

Soothing words, but apart from the fact that he was being economical with truth in claiming that Saudi Arabia was only a recent convert to fundamentalist Islam, there is little prospect of him carrying out his promise, considering how deeply entrenched Wahhabism is in Saudi DNA. The very political legitimacy of the House of Saud hangs on its 275-year-old pact with the Wahhabis. Under the 1744 pact between Muhammed Ibn Saud and Ibn Abd al-Wahhab, the founder of Wahhabism, Ibn Saud would protect and propagate the doctrines of the Wahhabi mission, while Ibn Abdul Wahhab would support the ruler, supplying him with 'glory and power.' Wahhabism propagates a literalist interpretation of the Quran and strict monotheism, rejecting such widespread Sunni practices as the veneration of saints and visiting their tombs and shrines.

Even at the height of his powers, Mohammed Bin Salman, or MBS, as he is commonly known, would have struggled to tinker with the foundations of the House of Saud, and at best he may have tried to open up Saudi society culturally to claim success for his "modernization" project. Even that now looks less likely in the light of his diminished stature after the heightened scrutiny of his disastrous military adventure in Yemen and the controversy over his alleged role in the brutal murder of the dissident Saudi journalist Jamal Khashoggi in October 2018. Jamal was killed inside the Saudi consulate in Istanbul allegedly by a hit squad sent from Riyadh and close to MBS.

What all this boils down to is that the military defeat of IS and its fellow or rival jihadis doesn't mean that it is the end of the road for extremist Islam, however much moderates might like to believe that they have won. Far from winning, they haven't even started to grasp the nettle. In order to win, they must first acknowledge the problem: that there *is* such a thing as an extremist strand of Islam, and that it *is* a mainstream thing—not a fringe phenomenon or an aberration that will go away without a fight.

The challenge before them is to defeat the obscurantist ideology that provides oxygen to extremists. Backed by powerful patrons, it is preached daily in thousands of mosques and madrasas across the world; and disseminated to millions of homes in Asia, Africa, Europe and the Middle East via sermons by TV evangelists like Zakir Nayak who the Saudis honoured with the prestigious King Faisal International Prize for his 'services to Islam.' It also flourishes on the American and European university seminar circuit where foreign extremist preachers regularly address Muslim students mobilized by local Islamic groups. Almost every British university has one or more Islamic student groups, often with links to radical organizations. In his memoirs, *The Islamist*, Ed Husain, an ex-radical, has detailed how he was radicalized by such groups as a student at a British university. Even prisons are not immune. Independent surveys in Britain have described prisons as breeding grounds for radicalization. The power of extreme Islamism has proved to be stronger than the fear and trauma of incarceration.

According to Sara Khan, who advises the British Government on its counter-terror strategy, 'spread of extremist ideas and behaviours among serving prisoners' is a big issue. Individuals are becoming more extremist in prisons. There are also fears about what happens when prisoners who advocate extremist beliefs and behaviour—whether Islamist or far-right supporters—are released into our communities.' (*The Independent*, 25 September, 2018)

Research shows that attempts to isolate suspected extremists by putting them behind bars have not worked. Nor has fear of incarceration deterred others from taking the plunge.

Contrast this aggressive and motivated campaign with the

muted response of moderates who, despite being in a majority, have been left wringing their hands. And this is particularly true of India. Most Islamic student bodies in Indian universities are run or dominated by fundamentalists unchallenged by an alternative secular discourse. Groups like the Students Islamic Movement of India (SIMI) have flourished because there is nobody to challenge them. Even when moderates care to intervene, their response seldom goes beyond a general denunciation of extremism but without offering an alternative and more positive vision of Islam. If I were a vulnerable 18-year-old courted by extremists and bombarded with powerful extremist messages, but nobody to counter them, what would I do? Except to drift towards those trying to court me? It is a point not often recognized that most young Muslims drift towards extremism simply by default: nobody else seems to want them. Moderates are missing in action.

Meanwhile, MBS's promise notwithstanding, there is no likelihood of Saudis abandoning Wahhabism anytime soon and with liberals, especially in South Asia, not quite able to get their act together for reasons ranging from a sense of complacency that the storm will blow over, to a certain defensiveness in the face of widespread Islamophobia, the road back from jihad to ijtihad is likely to be a very long one. Once again, as so often in Islam's history, the ideology that has the blessings of the rulers is winning. In this case, the ideology is Salafism, and the rulers, the House of Saud. Global Islam is in the grip of a process of Saudization,—a term used by British-Pakistani scholar Farzana Shaikh to describe the situation in Pakistan (*Making Sense of*

Pakistan, Preface to the second edition, 2018) And unless that stops, the crisis in Islam will continue. The following quote from the book about sums up both the cause of crisis and the solution:

> ...it was in Saudi Arabia that Salafism began, and it is in Saudi Arabia that it needs to be uprooted. The 1749 alliance between the Saudi royal family and Wahhabi clerics must be nullified. Without Saudi Arabia as a financial, educational and preaching base, the Salafi-Wahhabi could not survive on the fringes of the Muslim world. Before it takes hold of other capitals, Salafi-Wahhabism must be brought to an end. Its backwardness is not limited to creed, conduct and hardline conservatism. Its violence did not end in 1932 with the creation of Saudi Arabia, but erupts today with international jihadism.
>
> (*The House of Islam: A Global History,* Ed Husain)

I rest my case.

6

TRAPPED IN MENTAL GHETTOS

A relatively liberal Muslim friend—a respected Urdu journalist with inside track of the Muslim community—told me during one of our conversations that if ever there was a renaissance in Islam, 'it will be led by Indian Muslims.' What, I asked him, was the basis for his optimism? He replied: 'Look how sensibly and responsibly they behaved in the aftermath of the Babri Masjid demolition, and have not been provoked by all this Muslim-bashing that is going on.'

I wanted to pinch myself to make sure that I heard it right. Later, I heard almost exactly the same line from other liberal Muslims. The problem is that they are confusing a restraint induced by fear and insecurity for a sudden dawn of liberalism. No doubt, by and large, the community has displayed uncharacteristic restraint in the face of some pretty nasty provocations, but to deduce from this that it is in the midst of a renaissance is fantasy. The reality is that it had no other option but to lie low when the alternative—any act of bravado—risked inviting lynch mobs. Its 'responsible' behaviour is nothing but simply a result of its survival instinct. Which, no doubt, is an admirable advance on the politically suicidal strategies it has pursued in the past, including over the Babri Masjid dispute.

Much of the history of Indian Muslims since Independence has been a history of what may be called institutional illiberalism because of historically low levels of illiteracy; deep-seated conservatism; and a lack of enlightened leadership. It is not so much religious fundamentalism that is a problem (by and large Indian Muslims have escaped extremism) as is a closed mind, principally because of historical, social and cultural backwardness. Which was then exploited by a cabal of mullahs and Muslim 'leaders' who had a stake in keeping them backward. To compound matters, attempts by moderate Muslims to raise consciousness were very deliberately undermined by Hindu communalists who had their own reasons to see that Muslims remained insecure and behind purdah, as it were. By pulling down the shutters and retreating deeper and deeper into a shell, instead of trying to find a way to improve their situation, they played into the hands of the forces both within and outside the community who benefitted from their sense of insecurity and cultural impoverishment.

Zakia Soman of the pro-reform Bharatiya Muslim Mahila Andolan points out that Indian Muslims and their leadership remain 'mired in conservatism and short-sightedness around perceived religious issues.'

> They have not fully comprehended the idea of citizenship in a secular democracy, comprising rights and duties emanating from the Constitution. I have witnessed this gap in the understanding of several leaders during the course of my work following the Gujarat (2002) and Muzaffarnagar (2013) riots. The idea of demanding accountability from state institutions and simultaneously fulfilling one's obligations as citizen remains distant to a leadership obsessed with religious conservatism. Ordinary Muslims pay a price for this lack of vision. On the one hand, there are no means of a democratic participation and on the other hand, there is increased stereotyping. The irresponsible statements and unjust positions from religious leaders, such as around triple talaq, are highlighted, leading to cause further polarization in society. This leads to a situation where there is little awareness about the condition of ordinary Muslims and nobody cares for the absence of Muslims in a crowded public discourse.

(*The Indian Express*, 11 December, 2018)

The cumulative result is an insecure, stagnant, sullen, intolerant and leaderless community at risk of being targeted by global extremists who feed on frustrated Muslim youth. Luckily, we have managed so far to keep them at bay and I am often surprised how, but the old reserves of moderation and liberal thought that shaped the nineteenth and early twentieth century Indian Islam, are beginning to dry up. Mind you, there have been no significant reforms for close to a hundred years and we are running virtually on Empty. The only thing that has intensified is what Francis Robinson described as a unique feature of Indian Islam: the 'intensity of Indian Muslims' self-conscious identity.' (*Islam, South Asia and the West*, 2007, cited by Mushirul Hasan in *Moderate or Militant: Images of India's Muslims*, 2008)

In the interest of historical perspective, it is important to point out that in the nineteenth and early twentieth century, Indian Islam boasted of some very distinguished reform-minded Muslim thinkers such as Sir Syed Ahmed Khan, Maulavi Mumtaz Ali Khan, Maulavi Chiragh Ali and Justice Ameer Ali. They publicly opposed religious orthodoxy and what they regarded as obscurantism dressed up as tradition. Remarkably, all were devout practising Muslims, most of whom had beards. They were a living repudiation of the tendency to see every religious Muslim as a fundamentalist.

They were part of a mini-renaissance in global Islam in early twentieth century. British Islamic scholar Karen Armstrong has noted that 'nearly every leading intellectual in the Islamic world was a liberal.' And they outnumbered the fundamentalists. But that was then. Somewhere along the way, the clock stopped and it shows no sign of starting up again.

Several reasons are given for this atrophy. The most widely

held view attributes the decline of liberal-thinking Indian Muslims to the Partition which saw the educated, aspirational Muslim middleclass move to Pakistan, leaving behind mostly the uneducated and socio-economically backward Muslims who became fodder for self-styled conservative leaders in the absence of enlightened leadership. The other kind of Muslims who stayed back were the Marxist variety—disconnected from the community and unwilling to soil their hands by getting involved in its problems. The leadership vacuum was filled by mullahs and their political patrons, mostly Congressmen. To set the record straight, there did exist a small non-Marxist liberal elite, but slowly it vanished and was replaced by an illiberal and reactionary leadership, helped in no small measure by the Hindu Right. Both the Muslim and Hindu Right had a vested interest in keeping Muslims backward and have been feeding on each other to ensure that.

But 70 years after Partition this explanation has started to wear thin. Since then, a new generation of educated Muslim middle class—admittedly small—has emerged, with a fair sprinkling of well-heeled professionals including women; the stranglehold of mullahs has eased; and the community has become smarter in making political choices. But the greater social mobility and political awareness have not been matched by a change in attitudes which remain stuck in the past.

Liberal Muslim scholars like the late Mohammed Mujeeb (a leading educationist and the longest-serving Vice-chancellor of Jamia Millia Islamia), wanted Muslims to get out of their mental ghettos and 'make the most of their potential,' according to Mushirul Hasan.

> To scholars like Mujeeb, the choices were simple enough: if Islam is suspended between adjustment to ongoing change and resistance to the needed accommodation, Muslims... would be required to shun obscurantism and take their distinct values...into the mainstream of political life. They could no longer subscribe to the infallibility of established dogma; instead they would be expected to awaken once more the spirit of conscientious objection to prejudice, shake off the shackles of the past, and create a social order conducive to the dignity of the common man and woman.
>
> (*Moderate or Militant: Images of India's Muslims*, Mushirul Hasan, 2008)

Similarly, Maulana Abul Kalam Azad, one of twentieth century's great liberal Muslim thinkers, put a lot of emphasis on investigating truth even if it meant questioning accepted beliefs when they appeared to be in conflict with rational thought. In his book, *Ghubar-e-Khatir*, he admitted that he nearly lost his belief on discovering 'mutually contradicting convictions and discrepant dogmas' in Islam but he persisted in seeking the truth by asking more questions and ultimately found the answers to satisfy his intellectual curiosity.

When Mujeeb urged Muslims to come out of their 'mental ghettos,' he was echoing Azad and other great Muslim reformers.

Unfortunately, the Muslim community has slipped deeper into the quagmire of mental ghettos. At the heart of the problem is a huge intellectual vacuum allowing 'discrepant dogmas,' as Azad put it, to go unscrutinized. There aren't many influential Muslim public intellectuals, or Muslim think-tanks promoting liberal ideas. While researching this book, I asked almost every Muslim I met if they could name just five living liberal Muslim intellectuals, and they all drew a blank. I am not suggesting that there is not a single liberal Muslim intellectual, but they are so few and far from the limelight, that you have to scratch your head to recall their names.

Historically, the study of Indian Islam has been a neglected area. '*Intellectuals in the Modern Islamic World* (Eds. Stephane A. Dudoignon, Komatsu Hisao and Kosugi Yasushi) carries chapters on Egypt, Morocco, Bosnia-Herzegovina, Saudi Arabia, China, Pakistan, and Japan but *none* (italics mine) on India,' noted Mushirul Hasan, pointing out that 'Indian Muslims survive on the margins of academic consciousness; nobody even notices their varied social life and organizations.' (*Moderate or Militant: Images of Indian Muslims*, 2008) Including, it seems, Indian Muslims themselves. Hasan was among the honourable exceptions. And those exceptions are becoming rarer as older progressive voices fade out, while no major new voices are emerging. There is a lot more work being done on Islam, including Indian Islam, in the West than in India. And it is not all about terrorism or jihad. Nor is it all Orientalist.

Similarly, the study of Islamic theology in India is rudimentary and generally confined to madrasas where young people—mostly from disadvantaged backgrounds—are simply taught to learn the Quran by rote in an atmosphere as insular as once existed in the cloistered Christian monasteries. Even courses in advanced theology are structured around the most dogmatic interpretation of Islam. The most sophisticated of madrasas can not conceal the culture of exclusion and phoney piety they foster. Hem Borker is a Delhi-based academic who spent some time at one of India's leading women's madrasas—Madrasa Jamiatul Mominat near Jamia Millia in Delhi—as part of her DPhil research on Indian madrasas at Oxford University. Her book, *Madrasas and the Making of Islamic Womanhood* (OUP, 2018), is an unapologetically sympathetic study of madrasas and their relevance to the Muslim community, particularly women.

But even Borker appears to cringe at the level of segregation and the chauvinistic Muslim male attitude towards women she found at madrasas, starting with the obstacles she faced getting access to them as a 'single Hindu researcher studying abroad.'

Even when she got permission, it was only restricted access, and she was forced to cover her head, and, like the students, prohibited from using mobile phone, laptop, camera or tape recorder. The dress code required girls at the madrasa to cover themselves from head to toe all the time so that no part of their body including hair was exposed. They lived isolated lives behind multiple layers of security, totally cut off from the outside world. Although they are taught to use computers, Internet use is banned. As are all 'means of entertainment' such as seeing movies or going out for meals.

> The madrasa environment was very different from anything that I had been exposed to in the course of my own education or professional experience as a social worker in educational settings.

She points out that she had worked with minority communities earlier, but had

> never engaged with an institution that is so Muslim, not just in terms of the student and staff composition, but also in its cultural norms, behavioural practices and ethos...zealously fenced, with multiple levels of security, which can be quite unwelcoming and intimidating.

> (*Madrasas and the Making of Islamic Womanhood*, 2018)

Their idea of 'appropriate behaviour' expected of a pious Muslim woman consigned the girls to the status of glorified slaves stripped of any right to individual freedom. The girls, curious about the outside world, would ask her things like, 'Do you wear cut sleeves; do you use make-up; do girls and boys live in the same place; do you sit next to boys; do you have male teachers' and so on.

More disturbing is the Muslim vision of 'an idealised normative Islamic womanhood.' The following extract that Borker reproduces from a brochure of a girls' madrasa in Moradabad is instructive because it reinforces—as Borker says—the nineteenth century notion of educated Muslim women. It reads:

> A girl will serve her husband and keep him happy by taking care of his various needs within the Shariah. With her technical and academic knowledge she can also help her husband with work, business and family. As a mother, (the) girl will be able to provide proper upbringing to her children and provide them with good morals, religious and modern education. She will be able to build a sound character in her children. All this will be possible because of the knowledge she has gained during her education. As a neighbour a ...girl is also equipped and trained to give the last bath before burial and perform proper funeral Islamic rituals.

Note that the emphasis throughout is on morals and religious piety and the entire purpose of education is reduced to making a Muslim woman a good housekeeper equipped to look after her husband, children and neighbours. There is no mention of education as a source of knowledge and an agent of intellectual awakening. The author notes that during her research she was 'presented similar imagery of the ideal madrasa educated girl' by others.

Well, this doesn't look like the mindset of a community supposedly set to lead an Islamic Renaissance. Arguably, India's Muslim women are among the most oppressed, and no amount of moral equivalence pointing to repression of women in other communities, makes our own misogyny any less shameful. The Muslim attitude towards women is the more shameful considering Islam pioneered many of the rights they had not enjoyed before. Prophet Mohammad is known as a 'liberator' of women and recognized as 'feminist of his time' as Ed Husain writes in *The House of Islam*. He abolished infanticide; changed the rule on dowries so that the money went to the woman directly, and in the event of divorce, she retained her financial assets. For the first time, women were given the right to divorce their husbands and inherit property. I quote from the book:

'By the standards and in the context of the Prophet's time in seventh century Arabia, Muslims were among the most advanced communities in terms of recognizing women's human status and granting them rights.' How ironical then that 1400 years later Muslims are among the most backward in recognizing women's rights.

It is part of the steady drip, drip, drip with which the Muslim mind is closing, and slipping into illiberalism. There is really only one catch-all umbrella-yardstick to measure a liberal mindset: tolerance. It encapsulates everything that liberalism represents—secularism, free speech, individual freedoms, gender equality and the right lifestyle choices. I'm afraid most Indian Muslims fail to measure up to this yardstick. I can hear murmurs of 'but Muslims are not the only ones who are intolerant...' Which reminds me of Amitabh Bachchan's famous dialogue in *Deewar* justifying his criminal activities on similar grounds and challenging his critics before they could ask him to sign a confession:

'Haan, main sign karoonga; lekin pehle us aadmi ka sign le ke aao jisne mera baap ko chor kaha tha; pehle us aadmi ka sign le ke aao jisne meri maa ko gali deke naukri se nikal diya tha; pehle us aadmi ka sign le ke aao jisne mere haath pe ye likh diya tha...

Uske baad, uske baad mere bhai, tum jahan kahoge main wahan sign kar doonga.'

But on a more serious point, Muslim intolerance arising from faith-related sensitivities is much more widespread and deeply entrenched. India was the first country to ban Salman Rushdie's *The Satanic Verses* in 1988 at the instigation of its Muslim community. Not content with securing a ban claiming the book was blasphemous, its fundamentalist fringe went about attacking and intimidating anyone who dared to speak up for a writer's right to free speech. Late historian Mushirul Hasan was beaten up for simply suggesting that burning and banning books in the name of religious sensitivities was a bad idea. Even 26 years later, Muslims get worked up at the mere mention of Rushdie's name; he remains a persona non grata for Indian Muslims. As I have mentioned earlier, if there were a Rushdie test of tolerance, even many moderate Muslims would struggle to pass it.

Take the blasphemy issue. There was radio silence in India's Muslim community when Asia Bibi, a Pakistani Christian, was sentenced to death in 2010 on blasphemy charges. In 2018, a court exonerated her after a long legal battle, only to be confronted with lynch mobs threatening to kill her. Again, not a word of condemnation from Indian Muslims. As victims of majoritarian prejudices themselves, the least they could do was to show solidarity towards another member of a minority faith facing persecution next door.

'Deaf and dumb when it comes to a Christian, a Jew or a non-Muslim victim of injustice. How can this be explained?'

Kamel Abderrahmani, a Paris-based Algerian Muslim teacher wrote on Asianet.net news website questioning the silence of the Muslim world about Asia Bibi:

> Her sentence was similar to the one issued by the Islamic State group against Yezidis and Christians [In Iraq]. No one was outraged, no Muslim demonstrated in front of the embassy of that country. Is this a complicitous silence or just indifference? So many legitimate questions can be asked. Obviously, we do not ask much, just a minimum of solidarity towards a woman who continues to endure injustice, despite her acquittal…Today, so-called Muslim states, implicitly, embody intolerance towards religious minorities. In short, what Asia Bibi has experienced in Pakistan is what other non-Muslims experience in other Muslim countries. I am disappointed by the decadence and fundamentalism that affect the Muslim world whose essence and driving force are based unfortunately on a certain interpretation of religious texts.
>
> (The Silence of the Muslim World about Asia Bibi, 19 November, 2018)

The same 'decadence and fundamentalism' is evident in Indian Muslim attitudes towards Sharia or the Muslim Personal Law as it is known in India. While Sharia has been reformed in many Islamic countries, especially in relation to women's rights, it remains a no-go zone in India. Any suggestion for reform is seen by Muslims as a conspiracy to meddle in their religious affairs and to undermine their Islamic identity. The line is: Keep your hands off Sharia until the initiative comes from the community. Yet 70 years on since Independence, there is no sign of an initiative coming from the community.

'Since my student days, leaders have been using this alibi for not reforming Muslim law,' according to Tahir Mahmood, one of India's most authoritative voices on Islamic law. He argues that the Hindu law was reformed and codified between 1955 and 1956, despite resistance from Hindu religious circles. Similarly, the Christian divorce law of 1869 was liberalized by Parliament in 1991 in the face of opposition from church leaders. But Muslims have gotten away with it. It is not just the mullahs who are opposed to any tinkering with Sharia; even otherwise vocal moderates start to hedge their bets the moment you mention Muslim Personal Law. In private they agree that any radical social reform will have to be preceded by theological reforms, given that many of the more regressive social practices are sought to be justified by invoking Sharia. As an academic says, 'A liberalized Sharia is a precondition to any liberalization of Muslim society, but liberalization happens when the general climate in society is liberal and minorities feel confident.'

The problem with 'the-climate-is-not-right' narrative is that it is such old hat, it has started to seem like an excuse. As Dr Mahmood said: 'Since my student days, leaders have been using this alibi for not reforming Muslim law.' And it looks like we are going to hear more of this as the community seems to be in no mood to take the plunge. So, no green shoots of a renaissance any time soon.

Hope I am proved wrong.

7

SECULAR ISLAM IS A FANTASY

Modernizing Islam to make it fit for the twenty-first century is one of the most challenging and intensely debated issues of our time. And the good news is that outside the fundamentalist/extremist bubble there is hardly anyone who disputes that a liberal and secular Islam compatible with democracy will not only benefit Muslims but can be a force for good for the rest of the world too—as, indeed, it was before the collapse of the Ottoman Empire. The bad news, however, is that the consensus quickly breaks down when it comes to defining modern Islam. What should or would such an Islam look like? What bits ought it to give up in order to adapt itself to a sceptical, irreverent and individualistic age without losing its essence? What are the red lines? Can Sharia be amended? And what about the Quran? Is it open to reinterpretation to get around the ambiguities that have allowed sectarian interests to interpret it to serve their purpose?

Much of the debate is skewed by a profound misreading and misunderstanding about the nature of Islam, portraying it either as inherently liberal and inclusive; or irreversibly illiberal and exclusionist—a result of lazy assumptions and widespread ignorance on both sides of the liberal-conservative divide, particularly among Left liberal Muslims. For example, few are aware of the distinction between Islam and Islamism (political activism as manifested in the form of militant jihad and movements for the implementation of Sharia) and routinely conflate the two, describing Islamist terror as Islamic terror. Even within Islamism there are two strands: those who believe in achieving their aim through peaceful processes, and those who advocate violence. Mostly, it is the latter who set the agenda.

Prominent twentieth-century Islamists include Abul Ala Maududi, founder of Jamaat-e-Islami; Hasan al-Banna, founder of Muslim Brotherhood; Sayyid Qutb, a leading light of Egyptian Muslim Brotherhood and executed in 1966 for allegedly plotting to overthrow the then Egyptian President Gamal Abdel Nasser; and Ruhollah Khomeini, architect of the 1979 Islamic Revolution in Iran. It is important to point out that not all Islamists believe in violence. Violent extremists generally come from among Sayyid Qutb's followers.

SECULAR ISLAM IS A FANTASY

Historically, the liberal and fundamentalist Islam have been involved in a see-saw and often bloody battle for supremacy, and invariably—as discussed in the previous chapter—it is the foxy fundamentalists who have been able to seize the initiative, with ultra-conservationist Saudi Arabia setting the agenda for Muslims around the globe from the deserts of Arabia to Africa, Asia, Europe and the Americas. Its impact in the Middle East has been particularly toxic as illustrated by the rise of forces like al-Qaeda and IS. Robin Wright, a leading American commentator on Islam, has written that Islamist movements have arguably altered the Middle East more than any trend since the modern states gained independence, redefining 'politics and even borders.'

Against this backdrop, calls for modernizing Islam sound a bit too optimistic, especially when there is such lack of clarity and so much haziness around the notion of a 'modern' Islam. A glaring example of this haziness and one that illustrates the level of ignorance is the tendency to speak about modern or liberal Islam and a secular Islam in the same breath with one term being substituted for the other. They are presented as two sides of a coin. They are not. A liberal Islam is doable, as I have discussed earlier, and versions of it exist in several countries. But a secular Islam is an oxymoron. And here is why.

Secularism in its very elementary sense involves recognizing the public space as free from religion and neutral towards all religions, even if the State itself has religious characteristics such as in the case of Britain and America. Britain is a Christian

State characterized by different offshoots of Protestantism. All State rituals—opening of Parliament, start of the session in the morning, composition of the House of Lords, the monarch's obligation to protect Protestantism throughout the UK—are Christian. But public space in Britain is wholly secular. Christians don't get any preferential treatment; nor are Christian practices imposed on non-Christians; or in any area of public life.

Islam, however, doesn't recognize the idea of a secular public space. It is not meant as a criticism. That is how Islam was constructed. It is a bit like communism. Just as communism is all-pervasive in a communist State, so is Islam in an Islamic State. There is no such thing as a secular or neutral public space either in a communist or an Islamic State. Civil society is an extension of the State. That Islam and secularism are incompatible, is acknowledged by many authoritative scholars like Egypt's Yusuf al-Qaradawi who argue that Christianity is more comfortable with the idea of secularism because historically it has more or less maintained separation between State and religion.

> Islam's experience has indeed been the opposite, al-Qaradawi and others may argue. From its very beginning, Islam has provided a comprehensive guide regulating all aspects of life from birth until death, including those in the political sphere. From the times of Prophet Mohammad, through various regimes and caliphates, up to the modern period, it has maintained a close connection between the State and

religion. Most Muslims, at least in theory, have not accepted the idea of separation, particularly since non-separation has always been the norm.

(The Oxford Handbook of Secularism, Abdullah Saeed, 2007)

Leave alone an Islamic State, even in Muslim-majority States that don't formally call themselves Islamic, religion intrudes on public space in a way that it doesn't in non-Muslim majority States. This is true even of relatively liberal Muslim-majority countries such as Malaysia, Indonesia, Bangladesh and Turkey. They all impose some version of an Islamic code of conduct in the form of restrictions and prohibitions ranging from ban on alcohol consumption, selling or eating pork, ban on eating in public during Ramadan, dress code for Muslim women, and strict application of Islamic family laws for Muslims. In modern history, there are only two precedents of attempts to secularize a Muslim country, and both ended in tears. One is Turkey and the other, Iran.

Turkey was sought to be secularized by Mustafa Kemal Ataturk, hailed as the greatest Muslim modernizer of twentieth century, when after the collapse of the Ottoman empire he abolished the Caliphate and declared Turkey a modern republic. But in his zeal, he ended up effectively de-Islamizing Turkey by banning anything and everything in sight that had even a hint of Muslim or Islamic identity. Fez, the Turkish national headdress for men—a conical red cap with a black tassel on top—was replaced with Western-style brimmed hats, and burqa with skirt. Anyone found flouting the new dress code faced punishment. His goal, according to historians, was to completely rid Turkey of its Islamic past and convert it into a replica of modern European nations.

> In the next few years, he outlawed all Islamic schools, banned all Sufi orders, and closed down any society that had any Islamic identity. To mark the cultural shift, he replaced the Islamic calendar with the Gregorian one and the Arabic alphabet with the Latin one. The teaching of Arabic was banned, as was for a while in the 1930s, the performance of Turkish music...
>
> (*Islam Without Extremes: A Muslim Case for Liberty*, Mustafa Akyol)

Turkish historian Nur Yalman of Harvard University has likened Ataturk's push to secularize Turkey to Mao's disastrous Cultural Revolution.

Ataturk's was a demolition job, stripping Turkey of its Islamic heritage and character altogether. It provoked widespread protests, especially in Anatolia, which were put down with a heavy hand—like the response of today's Islamic fundamentalist authoritarian regimes to any dissent. This made even moderates wonder: if this is what modern and secular Islam looks like, do we really want it?

> For Muslims around the world, the secular model of secularism presented by the Turkish authorities implied the marginalization of the Sharia; a ban on public expression

of Islam, the prohibition of religious education for young Muslim children; restrictions on the use of the Arabic language, even in certain key rituals; and a ban on the headscarf and the veil for Muslim women, at least in public. This is how secularism looked, and for many Muslims it was shocking. They raised their voices to criticize it around the world. As a result, Turkish secularism has remained an oft-cited negative example of secularism in its most virulent form.

(Secularism, State Neutrality and Islam, *The Oxford Handbook of Secularism*, Abdullah Saeed, 2017)

Iran went through a similar process of aggressive secularization under Reza Shah Pahlavi, a policy that continued under his son Mohammad Reza Shah, the last Shah of Iran, until he was unceremoniously ousted in the 1979 Islamic Revolution led by Ruhollah Ayatollah Khomeini.

Like Ataturk, the Pahlavis seemed in a hurry to build a brand new Iran by ramming their vision of a secular State—stripping it of all vestiges of Islamic identity, including replacing traditional ways of dressing with western-style dresses. Ultimately both Ataturk and the Pahlavis came up against the limits of secularizing a Muslim society. Today, Iran is a repressive theocracy while Turkey under Recep Tayyip Erdoğan's soft Islamist Justice and Development Party has all but abandoned Kemalism and is competing with Saudi Arabia for supremacy in the Sunni Muslim world.

Nearer home, seventy years after its creation, Pakistan is still struggling to reconcile its Islamic identity with the supposed vision of its founder Mohammed Ali Jinnah which broadly envisaged an inclusive State that will be secular in its treatment of other faiths. According to British-Pakistani historian Farzana Shaikh, the idea of Pakistan remains deeply contested because it has not been able to resolve its deep identity crisis:

> At its heart lies the question of whether Pakistan was intended to secure a Muslim homeland free from the domination of a Hindu majority in independent India or whether it expressed a desire for a State informed by Islamic law where Parliament and the people would be subject to Divine injunctions mediated by a clerical elite...
>
> (*Making Sense of Pakistan,* Farzana Shaikh)

The crisis is starkly illustrated by Pakistan's prime minister Imran Khan's hybrid vision of Pakistan: a cross between Jinnah's idea of Pakistan and an Islamic State on the lines of the seventh century administration in Medina. In his victory speech after the 2018 elections, he declared that he wanted to build 'the kind of country that our leader Mohammed Ali Jinnah wanted' and the type of State established by Prophet Mohammad in the city of Medina.

Across the world, Muslim countries—and Muslim populations in non-Muslim countries—are wrestling with the question of reconciling Islam with democracy and modernity. This tension, I suggest, flows from the extraordinary intensity of Islam's relationship with its adherents. Of all the major faiths, Islam is unique in that it has a larger-than-life presence in the lives of its followers. If you are a devout Muslim it becomes an integral part of your daily life—from dawn to dusk—inseparable from your shadow.

> For the devout Muslim, Islam's divine touches leave an imprint on daily life...When a sincere believer awakes, she thanks God for bringing her a new day after a night's sleep. Throughout the day, in her standing, bowing, reciting, prostrating, and praising of God, she emulates the Prophet Mohamed. She puts on her slippers with her right foot first, as he did. In the bathroom, she enters first with her left foot, and brushes her teeth from right to left. She leads with her right foot after her ritual ablution and stands facing Mecca to pray. Everything from the halal breakfast to her choice of modest clothes is influenced by Islam, as explained in the Quran and lived by the Prophet.
>
> (*The House of Islam: A Global History,* Ed Husain)

The notion of a neutral or secular space doesn't exist for the devout Muslim. Public space becomes an extension of the mosque (a Muslim can offer namaaz anywhere—at the workplace, in a moving train, on roadside) and Muslimness comes to define them in relation to almost everything else.

In a 2007 Gallup poll, when asked about the importance of Islamic traditions and practices, an overwhelming majority of

Muslims said they mattered to them a great deal—ranging from 87 per cent in Egypt to 90 per cent in Turkey, 95 per cent in Saudi Arabia, and 96 per cent in Jordan.

In comparison, figures for Christians who said Christian customs and traditions were important to them was much smaller. These traditions and practices constitute the hallmark of Islamic identity and it is the fear of losing this identity that lies at the heart of Muslim wariness towards modernization, especially in the light of Turkish and Iranian precedents.

Islam's smothering presence in the lives of its adherents is also the reason why they react so strongly to any criticism of Islam. They see it as an attack on themselves, so deeply is their sense of their identity bound up with their religion. Islam means submission, and one is not regarded as a 'good' Muslim unless they have 'submitted' themselves to it fully. Hundreds of thousands of Muslims happily spend their life's savings at the cost of their other needs to perform Hajj even though it is not mandatory— being applicable only to those who are physically and financially able to do it.

Ali A. Rizvi, a Pakistani-American commentator, has described Islam as the 'central foundation' of a Muslim's daily existence and the Muslim community at large.

> In much of the Muslim world where I grew up, religion is more than just a belief system. It is inextricably embedded in every aspect of people's lives—it is the central foundation upon which family, community, and morality are built. And

perhaps of most consequence, it is intractably intertwined with one's very sense of identity.

(*The Atheist Muslim: A Journey From Religion To Reason*, Ali A. Rizvi)

Can this be reconciled with the idea of a secular Muslim society?

Turkish theologian, Mehmet Aydin, has said that Islam and the secular State are compatible as long as the latter respects religious freedom. It is a curious statement. Either he doesn't 'get' secularism, or he is being deliberately disingenuous. Secularism comes in different shapes. American secularism is not the same as British secularism; and French secularism is different both from American and British secularism. India has its own soft secularism: there is no explicit Constitutional separation between the State and religion (the word secularism wasn't even originally mentioned in the Constitution and was inserted only in the 1980s by Indira Gandhi.) Broadly, it allows freedom of worship to all citizens, and—on paper at least—the State is neutral in matters of faith and committed to treating all its citizens equally irrespective of religion, caste or creed, though it doesn't always work thus in practice.

But here is the critical bit: all the various forms of secularism share one important common characteristic: they all fulfil Mr Aydin's condition with regard to 'respect for religious freedom.' In fact, State neutrality vis-à-vis religion of its citizens and treating all equally without favouring one over the other lie at the heart of secularism. On the other hand, there is hardly any Muslim-majority State which 'respects' religious freedom, and treats religious minorities on an equal footing with Islam. So, it is Islam, or at least the way it is practised in Islamic and Muslim-majority States, which is at odds with secularism than the other way round.

To be sure, no faith looks kindly on secularism but most have adapted themselves to it while Muslims continue to drag their feet. Fundamentally because—as observed above—the idea of Islam as being omnipresent is an anti-thesis of secularism. Islam and secularism are a contradiction in terms. Secondly, secularism's association with the West and Christianity makes Muslims—even moderate Muslims—suspicious of it; and they see it as another Western conspiracy to undermine Islam. 'Even many Muslims who appear to be rather moderate on many political issues are very uncomfortable talking about secularism in a positive way. (Abdullah Saeed, *The Oxford Handbook of Secularism*, 2017)

Secular-scepticism is hardwired into the Muslim mind for a variety of theological and historical reasons. And until they are able to resolve this tension, a secular Islam will remain a fantasy.

8

WHY ARE YOUNG MUSLIMS LEAVING ISLAM

The Economist narrated the story of an American Muslim boy of Somali descent, Mahad Olad, whose immigrant parents tricked him into going on a holiday with them to Kenya where they had made arrangements for him to go to a seminary to 'restore' his failing faith in Islam. He had no idea about his parents' plans until he landed in Kenya.

As soon as he stepped off the plane on a family holiday to Kenya, Mahad Olad knew something was wrong. His mother, a 'very devout, very conservative, very Wahhabi' woman, was acting strangely—furtively taking phone calls when she thought he was out of earshot. His suspicions would soon be proved correct. Mr Olad's family, Somali immigrants to America and devout Muslims, had discovered that he had not only renounced Islam but was also gay. The holiday was a ruse, an intervention to save his soul.

(*The Economist*, 15 March, 2018)

When he got wise of their plan to hand him over to the care of Muslim clerics who would 'restore' his faith, he got so frightened that he managed to escape. 'In the dead of night he sneaked into his mother's room, stole his passport and was whisked away by taxi to the embassy, which eventually returned him safely to America. He has not spoken to his family since,' according to the above report.

Behind Olad's story hangs a tale we don't usually hear about: how Islam is facing a wave of desertion by young Muslims suffering from a crisis of faith. The story we normally hear is of an Islam growing from strength to strength, and how for all the phobia that exists around it, it remains the fastest growing religion with 1.6 billion followers across the world and acquiring new converts on an almost daily basis. What we don't hear is that it is also being abandoned by moderate Muslims, mostly young men and women, ill at ease with growing extremism in their communities. The ranks of ex-Muslims is reported to be swelling. 'As the number of American Muslims has increased by almost 50 per cent in the past decade, so too has the number of ex-Muslims,'

The Economist report said, citing a Pew Research Centre survey according to which 23 per cent of Americans raised as Muslims no longer identify with the faith. Most are young second-generation immigrants, but there are also older Muslims 'married to devout Muslim spouses and driving children to the mosque to study the Koran, at weekends to cover up their apostasy.'

And it is not just an American or Western phenomenon. Even deeply conservative countries with strict anti-apostasy regimes like Pakistan, Iran and Sudan have been hit by desertions. The Saudis were taken aback when the American journal, *The New Republic*, revealed the scale of Muslim conversion to atheism in their country, and more widely in the Muslim world. The numbers were eye-popping, ranging from hundreds to thousands in some countries. The Editor-in-chief of FreeArabs.com says:

> When I recently searched Facebook in both Arabic and English, combining the word 'atheist' with names of different Arab countries I turned up over 250 pages or groups, with memberships ranging from a few individuals to more than 11,000. And these numbers only pertain to Arab atheists (or Arabs concerned with the topic of atheism) who are committed enough to leave a trace online.'
>
> (Invisible Atheists, Ahmed Benchemsi, *The New Republic*, 24 April 2015)

The journal cited a 2012, WIN/Gallup International poll which found that 5 per cent of Saudi citizens—more than a million people—self-identified as 'convinced atheists,' the same percentage as in the United States. '19 per cent of Saudis—almost six million people—think of themselves as "not a religious person." In Italy, the figure is 15 per cent. These numbers are even more striking considering that many Arab countries, including Saudi Arabia, the United Arab Emirates, Sudan and Yemen, uphold the Sharia rule punishing apostasy with death,' it pointed out.

It is claimed that the atheist-scientist Richard Dawkin's *God Delusion* is the most downloaded book in the Middle East, particularly in Saudi Arabia. It is now being translated into Arabic and there are plans to offer it free to Arab readers. The trend is catching on despite the fact that in many Islamic countries, apostasy is punishable by death. Most Islamic countries oppose the universal declaration of human rights and have refused to sign it because it provides for the 'freedom to change religion or belief.'

The exact figure of former Muslims may never be known as most remain in the shadows to avoid detection. Those who have 'outed' themselves say they live in permanent fear for their own lives and safety of their families. In Pakistan, preachers have called for the houses of apostates to be burned down. They communicate through anonymous online forums claiming tens of thousands of followers, and loose global networks under the umbrella nomenclature, 'Ex-Muslims' and 'Muslim-ish.' A Twitter campaign in Britain in 2015, had thousands of ex-Muslims from across the world tweeting their reasons for choosing to abandon their faith. These ranged from intolerance and inferior status of women to absence of freedom of thought and the idea of immutability of a seventh century doctrine. One -@Lib Muslim wrote: #ExMuslimBecause Misogyny, homophobia, stoning people to death, and killing apostates don't suddenly become "respectable" when put in a holy book. (Ali A. Rizvi, *Huffington Post*, 23 November, 2015)

Oxford University academic Faisal Devji has argued that by retaining 'Muslim' in their name, 'ex-Muslims are recognizing the theological character of their renunciation.'

> The Muslims among whom I was raised in East Africa included many who refused to pray or fast and were openly critical of religion. It would never occur to them to renounce Islam and proclaim atheism as a new identity or mission, which would have catapulted them back into a theological narrative.

(Conversions from Islam in Europe and Beyond, Faisal Devji, *The New York Times*, 15 April, 2017)

Simon Cottee, a British academic, has documented stories of many former Muslims in *The Apostate: When Muslims Leave Islam*. In each case, reasons for their decision differ, varying from religious bigotry and oppression, to violence in the name of Islam. Sometimes, as *The Economist* wrote in the 15 March, 2018 report, it could be a reaction to certain Quranic verses or the Hadith—the sayings of the Prophet Mohammad. 'Often the verses that trigger this are controversial ones about slavery or gender that family members and imams cannot explain satisfactorily. Coming across the writings of Ayaan Hirsi Ali, Richard Dawkins or Christopher Hitchens sometimes has the same effect. Some chafe at sexism or homophobia,' it reported.

According to Faisal Devji,

> Whether the converts are repulsed by the violent forms Islam has taken in places like Syria and Afghanistan or are backing up their claims for asylum, the conversions occur quietly and rarely as a result of proselytism. Nor do they tend to be accompanied by any transformation in the appearance, behavior or language of the convert. Analyzing the news reports suggests that these conversions are characterized by multiple quotidian and ambiguous motives. (*New York Times*, 15 August, 2017)

Brian Whitaker, a noted Middle East correspondent and the author of *Arabs Without God*, debunks the explanation that the phenomenon is a reaction to the violent acts being perpetrated in the name of Islam.

> While researching my book...I spent a lot of time trying to find out why some Arabs turn to atheism and none of those I spoke to mentioned terrorism or jihadism as a major factor...
> That is not particularly surprising, because atheism is a rejection of all forms of religion, not just the more outlandish variants of it.

Benchemsi in his Invisible Atheists, *New Republic* article

mentioned earlier, pointed out:

> For the vast majority of Arab atheists, the road to disbelief begins…with personal doubts. They start to question the illogicalities found in the holy texts. Why are non-Muslims destined to hell, even though many of them are nice, decent people? Since God knows the future and controls everything, why would he put some people on the wrong path, then punish them as if he had nothing to do with their choices? Why is wine forbidden, yet virtuous Muslims are promised rivers of it in heaven?

Walking By Moonlight: My Journey Out Of Islam is an extraordinary account of how a devout young Muslim woman turned her back on Islam after intense contemplation. She published an anguished Open Letter in *The Ex-Muslim*, a North American journal (27 January, 2017) detailing her painful journey to atheism. For fear of reprisal, she identified herself simply as Amira, a medical professional from Texas. The following is her story; I am discussing it at length because it will resonate with millions of rational and questioning Muslims everywhere. It can be any thinking-believer's story:

In her open letter, she wrote that she was born and raised as a practising Muslim. She wore hijab, and at one point even the full-face niqab. She was 'obsessed' with her faith and wanted to be an Islamic scholar. Her 'existence' centred around Islam and she aspired to be recognized as the 'best Muslim' around. She taught Quran to others and shared her knowledge of Islam with fellow Muslims who were less knowledgeable, but as she delved deeper, she started to develop doubts. There were aspects of Islam that she found hard to reconcile with. She stated,

> I am not someone who takes things blindly. If something is going to dictate every aspect of my life, then I demand indisputable perfection and sensibility in it. I don't want to believe in Islam because I'm told to or was raised to, but because I have analyzed it and it passes every test. In fact, the Quran encourages us to critically analyze the religion. So I took my religion and my efforts to understand it very seriously.

First she dismissed the doubts, believing that Allah was 'testing' her. 'The Quran warns that we will be tested in faith through wealth, loss, health, etc. I was convinced my test was psychological because of my covertly shaky spirituality and nagging questions,' she wrote. But she continued to be nagged by doubts and consulted scholars and imams. They told her that she was 'over-analyzing' and should stop asking too many questions. 'I was even told that *Shaytaan* (the devil) was hindering my understanding.' That was the last straw. She concluded that she could not honestly continue to follow a faith she didn't fully believe in, and decided reluctantly to leave the faith.

It is important to note that it was only when she didn't find the answers to her questions that she decided to leave the fold. This in fact is a significant common thread running through most of the accounts of ex-Muslims I've read: that it was NOT an easy decision to make. Some mulled for years before they were able to make up their minds as they struggled to reconcile what they saw as the contradictions between all the nice things they were taught about Islam and how it was actually practised. Before jumping ship, most apostates claim they made sincere efforts to clarify their doubts and overcome their scepticism— some learned Arabic and went back to original texts to make sure for themselves that they hadn't got it wrong. It was only when—on the basis of their own independent reading of the scriptures—they concluded that they could not honestly continue to cling on to their faith, that they reluctantly took the plunge.

Many are said to suffer intense emotional and psychological trauma afterwards in a sign of how strongly Muslims feel about their religious identity, and Islam's dominant presence in their lives, as I have already discussed. The loss of that identity leaves them in a social and moral limbo. There is at least one documented case of suicide—a young British Muslim, Irtaza Hussain, felt so disorientated and depressed that he went to seed and ultimately took his own life.

The trend has been described as a 'ticking bomb' with a new generation of educated Muslims starting to question the fundamentals of their faith.

In his book, *Islam Without Extremes: A Muslim Case for Liberty*, Turkish writer Mustafa Ayokal poses the question that, he says, 'haunts the minds of millions of my co-religionists: Is Islam a religion of coercion and repression? Or is it compatible with the idea of liberty...?'

For the first time, the narrative that it is not Islam but its perverse interpretation that is the problem, is being questioned. According to ex-Muslims, Islam cannot escape blame completely for what is being done in its name: the verses cited by jihadi groups to justify their actions do exist—and no attempt has been made to expunge them or contextualize them, the rationale being that divine revelations are 'immutable.'

Ali A. Rizvi, a US-based Pakistani writer, describes his own dispiriting experience of how he came to lose his faith after wrestling with his doubts for many years. Son of a Pakistani diplomat, he spent most of his adolescent years in several Islamic countries, including Saudi Arabia. He was hit by the gap between the benign Islam taught to him by his upper-middleclass liberal parents and the hate and prejudice-filled Islam practiced in the land of its birth. What really annoyed him was the hypocrisy that, he believes, characterizes the debate on Islam in Muslim communities whereby, while Islam is given credit for a personal achievement or 'good' deeds of a Muslim, it is promptly exonerated of any responsibility for their 'bad' deeds with the standard response: 'This has nothing to do with Islam.'

> Since childhood, I have heard examples of the great scientific and mathematical discoveries of Muslim scientists...during Islam's 'golden age.' The achievements of these men were truly revolutionary, but had as much to do with Islam as Christianity had to do with the achievements of Newton, or Judaism with the achievements of Einstein...Where there

is no direct link, as with Islam and scientific achievement, every attempt is made to try and establish one. But when there is a direct link between scripture and action—as in the case of jihadi violence, or hitting one's wife—it is not only denied, but those who point out are labelled ignorant, or even bigoted.

(*The Atheist Muslim: A Journey from Religion to Reason*, Ali A. Rizvi)

To put it in perspective, though, some of the arguments of ex-Muslims including Ali's, appear disingenuous. The Muslim defensiveness is certainly an issue but which faith and its followers—Christians, Jews, Hindus, Sikhs—don't become defensive when attacked? Catholic Church is openly homophobic and misogynistic, and regards it as its mission to 'civilize' people of other faiths; Hinduism has an oppressive caste system that has echoes of apartheid, and when it comes to homophobia and misogyny it is as bad as Islam; Judaism is intolerant not only towards people of other faiths but even towards liberal Jews. Yet, you will find few Catholics, Hindus or Jews who would not insist that theirs is the most peaceful and tolerant faith; and those who do nasty things in its name are not 'true' Catholics/Hindus/Jews.

But that is another debate. Coming back to the crisis in Islam, I wish I could explain it in terms of the broader crisis of faith in all religions, marked by an alarming fall in Church attendance in the West, and the general growing agnosticism among the young around the world. Islam's is not a crisis of faith; or it wouldn't be the fastest growing religion (even those who have left it say they wish they hadn't.) Its crisis emanates from a very simple fact: its contested doctrine of immutability—the belief that Islamic teachings with all its verbal and structural ambiguities are Allah's final word and cannot be tampered with even for the purpose of preventing their abuse by sequencing and contextualizing them so that they are are not torn out of context to justify misdeeds in the name of Islam. Consequently, a once young, dynamic and progressive religion has started to look its age—and out of step with the demands of the modern age. Worse, you are not allowed to ask any questions: Islam comes as a take-it-or-leave-it package. Dissent is not only frowned upon but can have consequences if you live in a Muslim country. Even in liberal milieus, asking questions about or expressing scepticism over scriptural claims is a no-no. Parents shrug these off and tell you to move on. Now if you're a young Muslim who has been brought up in a liberal atmosphere and taught to be curious and ask questions if you've doubts about anything, you begin to wonder why you are being stonewalled, why is it that your normally open parents suddenly become cagey when queried about Islam? What's going on?

It is these young Muslim men and women who, out of sheer frustration, are abandoning Islam.

Admittedly, there is no way to verify all of ex-Muslims' accounts or the real scale of the phenomenon, but even allowing for exaggeration, it doesn't make a pretty picture. With extremists flourishing and moderates getting squeezed out, Islam's existential crisis can only get worse in the coming years.

9

AT THE BOTTOM OF THE HEAP

Any reference to the Arab world is invariably preceded by the superlative adjective oil-rich, conjuring up the image of a prosperous, educated and contented people. This, however, couldn't be farther from reality. And the reality is this: Much of the Muslim world is socially illiberal. Most Islamic and Muslim-majority countries are not democracies. They are either repressive monarchies, one-party dictatorships or ruled by authoritarian figures with disdain for civil liberties and the rule of law.

The abortive Arab Spring—a series of anti-government protests and uprisings—that swept the Middle East in 2010, was a manifestation of repressed public anger against authoritarian and oppressive regimes in the region. Although the revolt fizzled out—it was suppressed with heavy force in most countries—the discontent that gave rise to it continues to simmer. Frustration over lack of political and social freedoms is exacerbated by economic deprivation, resulting in frequent eruption of street protests over price rises and youth unemployment.

Successive UN Human Development reports have found Arab countries doing badly on major development indices—reporting low life expectancy rates, high unemployment, vast economic inequality, poor education, and high levels of gender inequality. Nearly half of the 57 member States of the Organisation of Islamic Conference are classified by the World Bank among the least developed nations. (*Financial Times*, 14 January, 2008)

Take any economic indicator—industrial production, manufacturing output, GDP, technology—and you find the majority of Muslim countries struggling. No wonder, social discontent is high. The 2016 UN Arab Human Development Report warned that this frustration and anger was feeding radicalization among youth. It said the Arab youth could no longer be taken for granted. A failure to provide decent jobs for youth may fuel greater social and economic tensions in the region.

Sophie de Caen, Deputy Director of the Regional Bureau for Arab States in UNDP, commenting on the UN Arab Human Development Report said, 'Today, youth in the region are more educated, more connected and more mobile than ever before. Arab countries can reap the huge demographic dividend that its young population represents if they invest in enhancing the capacities of their youth and enlarging opportunities available to them.' In the words of former Malaysian Prime Minister Abdullah Ahmad Badawi: 'Large parts of the Muslim world are indeed among the most backward and economically underdeveloped.'

> Some Muslims have closed their minds and allowed the weight of tradition and narrow religious interpretation to stifle inquiry and innovation. Limiting knowledge to religious matters and an overemphasis on rote learning extinguishes the spirit of discovery. This is a disservice to Islam. Similarly, Muslims often forget that work is also a form of worship and that Islam calls for diligence and industry. The Muslim world will progress farthest when it unlocks and develops this potential, through quality education at all levels. Moreover, this will never be achieved if some Muslims continue to neglect the right to education and work for women. Women constitute half the Muslim world's human capital and in marginalizing women we only impoverish ourselves.'
>
> (*Financial Times*, 14 January, 2008)

It is notable that while the global Muslim community accounts for some 20 per cent of the world's population, it contributes only 5 per cent of the world's income. Poverty, illiteracy and inequality dog many parts of the Muslim world. Some countries are so poor that they rely on Western handouts. Muslim communities—

wherever they live, including India—lag behind in economic and educational fields. This is as much true of Muslim communities in developing countries as of those settled in developed Western societies. In Britain, Muslims are among the most economically and educationally backward groups.

British rights activist Sara Khan, in the book, *The Battle for British Islam*, writes: 'Unemployment is higher among Muslims than any other religious group and particularly among women.' Also, over the past two decades, British Muslims have 'become ever more conservative on social and equality issues.' A trend visible in India too. Muslims in non-Muslim countries tend to blame their economic and educational backwardness on communal/racial discrimination which they argue denies them opportunities available to others. To some extent it is true; the system is not only not on their side, but, in some cases, actively works against them. In India, the institutional bias Muslims face has been comprehensively documented by the Sachar Committee headed by late Delhi High Court Chief Justice Rajinder Sachar, in its 2006 report.

But surely this cannot be the sole reason because other minority groups do manage to forge ahead despite such hurdles. In most Western countries, Hindu minority groups are way ahead of their Muslim peers both economically and in education. Which raises the question: If they can do it despite all the discrimination and bias, why not Muslims? One reason is a general lack of aspiration derived from a sense of victimhood which then allows them to blame others—society, system, etc.—

for their own failures.

But a more fundamental issue, as the controversial Somali-Dutch activist Ayaan Hirsi Ali in her book, *Heretic*, argues, is the 'tension' between Islam as it is practised and modernity. Especially where Islam is in a minority, Muslims are 'engaged in a daily struggle,' she says, to reconcile themselves to demands of a secular and pluralistic society that 'challenges their values and beliefs at every turn.' 'Many are able to resolve this tension only by withdrawing into self-enclosed (and increasingly self-governing) enclaves. This is called cocooning, a practice whereby Muslim immigrants attempt to wall off outside influences, permitting only an Islamic education for their children and disengaging from the wider non-Muslim community.'

Normally, I don't take Ali seriously because of her dubious role in inflaming Islamophobia (*Heretic*, too, I find riddled with sweeping and often misleading generalizations) but she is absolutely right about the Muslim 'struggle' with Western-style secularism and pluralism—and how they react to it. Ghettoization, it seems, is more widespread among Muslims than other faith groups, including in India. Surveys in the West have shown Muslim communities living 'parallel lives' practically cut off from the wider community. It should be pointed out that not all of it has to do with Islam; there are a variety of reasons for Muslim ghettoization, including threat to their security. Or being denied housing in mixed areas, as in India. But, yes, Muslims do have a problem with integration and adapting to modern ideas that they, often mistakenly, believe are not sanctioned by Islam.

Talking about ideas, the modern Muslim world is virtually at a standstill with almost zero contribution to arts and sciences. The few individual Muslims who have made a mark, all live in the West. Zakri Abdul Hamid, Malaysia's prominent academic and a former member of the UN Secretary-General's Scientific Advisory Board, points out: 'Of the three Muslim Nobel Prize recipients, all made their mark while working in industrialized countries. The knowledge-based economy predicated on science, technology and innovation (STI) is still an elusive dream for most parts of the Muslim world.' (*New Straits Times*, 9 April, 2018)

Books don't sell in the Arab world. Its glitzy malls sell everything else under the sun but books—because, apparently, there is no demand for them. Figures show that book sales in the region are about the lowest in the world. The average print run of a successful book is estimated to be between 1,000 to 3,000 copies. In an article, Why Don't Arabs Read? (Al-Fanar Media site, 7 July 2016) Cairo-based commentator Ursula Lindsey cited a report presented at the Frankfurt Book Fair in 2013 which estimated that the Arab world, with its population of over 362 million people in 2012, produced about the same number of books as Romania with a population of 21.3 million and Ukraine 45.6 million, in 2012.

It is attributed to a combination of widespread illiteracy (despite an improvement in literacy rates in the past decade, more than one-third of youth remain illiterate; in Egypt a quarter of the population was illiterate in 2013) and a lack of reading culture at home. Most Arab households simply don't have books.

'In households where television reigns supreme, where an older generation may well be illiterate or barely literate, and where one encounters books in school as material to be memorized, is it any surprise that reading is viewed as a chore?' asks Lindsey in the same article.

Lack of a reading culture among Muslims is ironic. Because the very first words that Gabriel spoke to Prophet Mohammad when he appeared to him on Mount Hira was to command him to read. Mohammad replied: 'I am not a reader. I don't read.' To which Gabriel said: 'Read in the name of your Lord who created you.' Islam puts a great deal of stress on learning and knowledge. I grew up hearing that Islam commands Muslims to seek knowledge from wherever they can get it—even if it means 'going to China'. To be an *aalim fazi*—learned and knowledgeable—was supposed to be sine qua non of a civilized Muslim.

Instead of building modern educational institutions, the Muslim world has been busy setting up madrasas funded by Arabs to propagate the most reactionary version of 'authentic' Islam. There has been an explosion of—mostly Saudi-funded—madrasas globally, including in India, producing semi-literate 'scholars' fed on a hardline interpretation of Islam. These have been described as 'nurseries' for extremists. The Taliban (literally meaning students) are a product of these seminaries, and so are most of the extremists operating in Pakistan. Masood Azhar, the alleged mastermind behind the 2008 Mumbai attack and the 2019 Pulwama attack, runs a string of madrasas where vulnerable young men are indoctrinated. After the Pulwama incident,

Pakistani authorities raided a number of them in Bahawalpur, Muridke and Lahore.

In Islamabad, Pakistan's capital, there are more madrasas than mainstream educational institutions, The Gulf News (13 March, 2019) reported, citing a survey. It said the survey conducted in 2017 showed that in Islamabad 'the federal government has not opened a new conventional school since 2013, while religious seminaries or madrasas keep mushrooming in the region.'

'There are roughly 425 madrasas operating in the federal capital and a majority of them are unregistered,' the data shows.

In India, too, madrasas are taking the place of mainstream Muslim education, especially in smaller towns and poorer neighbourhoods. Many have been found to be preaching Wahhabi extreme version of Islam and have become recruiting centres for potential extremists. Aided by hawala funding from petro-dollar-rich Gulf countries, these seminaries were found to be indoctrinating young impressionable minds, according to an India Today survey of madrasas in Kerala, published in January 2018.

The point is that far from liberalizing and going forward, Muslims are actually regressing and losing touch with Islam's original spirit. A faith whose very raison d'etre was rooted in a progressive vision—to show light to a people steeped in the darkness of illiteracy and superstition—has become an antithesis of its own founding philosophy. Today, Islam is commonly linked to backwardness, intolerance, status quo-ism, misogyny—and of course, terror.

AT THE BOTTOM OF THE HEAP

> What images are conjured today by the word 'Islam'? Walk into any bookstore, and you will initially be drawn to a stack of breathless titles that are truly frightening. These journalistic exposés reveal worlds of terrorist intrigue and plots against the United States. Alongside these potboilers are books...delivering with masterful condescension the verdict of failure upon Islamic civilization, and the promise of an apocalyptic clash between Islam and the West. Tucked into a corner one may find a few academic surveys of Islamic theology and history, written in the tedious and excruciating prose reserved for textbooks. There may also be a couple of apologetics written by Muslims, attempting to defend Islam against any accusations. Finally, and most impenetrable of all, there will be two or three translations of the Quran, a foreign text that remains an enigmatic and unreadable cipher. How can anyone make sense of all this?
>
> (*Rethinking Islam In the Contemporary World*, Carl W. Ernst)

It is when Islam and Muslims stop being defined by such images that we can claim to have made some progress. Alas, that seems a long, long way off.

10

LET US STOP BEING SO BORING AND PIOUS

I worry that Indian Muslims have become rather boring. Ask them out for a drink, and they will say, 'But I don't drink alcohol anymore.'

Offer to take them to the best steakhouse in town for a meal, and while you are having visions of delicious steak and chilled beer, they will say: 'I think, I'll stick to vegetarian and a Diet Coke.'

Why? Because they are not sure the meat served there is halal. Let us ask the chef, you suggest. 'No, No. I don't want to take any risk.'

Invite them to a party, and they will say: 'Thanks, but I'm not a party animal.'

Good Muslims don't do hedonism.

Funnily, among them are people I once used to hang around with at cocktail parties and barbeques where nobody cared where the meat came from. I moved to Britain about 20 years ago and during this period, it seems, the Muslim aesthetics has changed dramatically. The joie de vivre and spontaneity has lost out to a new self-conscious religiosity, and notion of Muslimness.

SO, WHAT HAPPENED?

You get different responses. Some try to make light of it: Been there, done that...time to come home. Some cite family pressure—a conservative nagging wife, or a newly-religious son. But most attribute it to a reaction to Islamophobia and demonization of Islam. Echoing the 'black is beautiful' campaign against racism, they say it is their way of reclaiming their faith and demonstrating pride in Muslim identity.

Even those who are not particularly religious in observing daily Islamic rituals have become socially more conservative in their lifestyle choices to mirror an Islamic or Muslim way of life. The idea of 'halal' and 'haram' has become deeply ingrained. To be *seen* to be a 'good' Muslim is the new aesthetics; so I don't drink because my faith doesn't permit it; I eat only halal because that is what my faith wants me to; I have a beard because that is what it says in the Quran or is in accordance with Hadith, etc.

Except that there is widespread ignorance about what is really considered halal and haram in Islam, contrary to what is generally assumed. There is a wrong assumption that anything not explicitly approved is prohibited. The fact is exactly the opposite, everything is permissible unless it is explicitly prohibited. There are four categories of dos and don'ts: Wajib: mandatory acts such as prayers; Makruh: better to avoid but not banned; Haram: specifically banned; Halal: explicitly permitted.

Guess what? Alcohol is not explicitly banned and according to British Muslim scholar Ed Husain, 'indeed some religious scholars and caliphs drank alcohol, and others did not.' (*The House of Islam: A Global History*) Similarly, contrary to claims, there is no Quranic mandate for men growing beards or women covering their hair.

'All these actions are derived from alleged sayings of the Prophet. Muslims have lost the courage to question Hadiths (the Prophet's sayings) that do not align with the Quran,' according to Husain.

So, a lot of modern Muslim piety has its origins in misreading. But, I suspect, it is also about virtue-signalling: Look at me, I am such a good Muslim. A way of shaming their more happy-go-lucky peers who might like an occasional drink and don't obsess about how the chicken they are eating was slaughtered. By now I've come to recognize the look on their faces when declining a drink: a mixture of superiority and condescension often laced with a sarcastic comment like: '*Aap peejiye, aap ko mubarak*' (you carry on, good luck.)

But jokes apart, a simple-to-follow faith with uncomplicated rituals and loads of exemptions and relaxations for those not able to perform them (you can do your namaaz sitting if you are not able to stand; if you miss a prayer, you can make up later) has been turned into a minefield of punitive prohibitions and commands. A 24/7 dawn-to-dusk preoccupation, with the Faithful supposed to be scrambling to comply with endless dos and don'ts (which foot to put on the floor first when you wake up in the morning, what to eat, what to wear) with many having their origins in Hadith of doubtful provenance.

Here it is important to make a distinction between religiosity as a spiritual experience and mere display of religious piety by flaunting symbols of Islamic identity.

Religiosity also has an intellectual dimension, according to Riaz Hassan, an internationally known Islamic scholar, who has done a comparative study of religiosity.

'The intellectual dimension refers to the expectation that religious persons will possess some knowledge of the basic tenets of their faith and its sacred scripture.' (*On Being Religious: Patterns of Religious Commitment in Muslim Societies*, Riaz Hassan, Institute of Defence and Strategic Studies, Singapore, 2005)

Public displays of piety are more about identity assertion mostly in a political context when the identity in question is seen to be threatened. Appearance—beard, hijab, off-booze, kosher meat, etc.—takes precedence over conviction. In the context of Indian Muslims' increasing tendency towards public show of piety, the following observation about Egypt a decade ago makes interesting reading:

> There is a strong undercurrent of competition in Egypt these days, an unstated contest among people eager to prove just how religious they are. The field of battle is the street and focus tends to be on appearance, as opposed to conviction. It is not that the two are mutually exclusive; but they are not necessarily linked. As Egyptians increasingly emphasize Islam as the cornerstone of identity, there has been a growing emphasis on public displays of piety. For women, that has rapidly translated into the nearly universal adoption of the hejab, a scarf fitted over hair and ears and wrapped around the neck....With that, religious symbols have become the fashion.

(*New York Times*, Michael Slackman, 12 Nov, 2007)

Sounds familiar?

As for Egyptians, so for many Indian Muslims 'religious symbols have become the fashion.' Yet, intriguingly, a majority of Muslims, I suspect, fail to carry out even mandatory obligations such as offering namaaz five times a day and fasting for the entire month of Ramzan. These are among practices known as Islam's Five Pillars. Most Muslims are occasional namaazis, generally offering namaaz on Fridays, Eid-ul-Fitr, Eid-uz-Zuha and other special occasions. Similarly, during Ramzan, the tendency is to cherry-pick days for fasting—generally the first roza of the month and the one that falls on the last Friday preceding the end of Ramzan—*al vida ka roza* (the farewell fast.)

This relaxed and practical attitude is a far cry from the image Muslims present of themselves with their public show of piety. Muslims complain, with some justification, of being caricatured and stereotyped—all beard, skullcap, and burqas—but they overlook their own role in contributing to these caricatures by constantly parading their Muslimness. As I have pointed out there is a big gap between their practical approach to religion and the impression they give to the outside world of a community consumed with religiosity.

Let us leave faux piety to the mullahs. Do grow a beard if you like, wear a hijab if you like, stay off booze if you like (because too much of it gives a hangover, anyway) but *Allah ke Waste* don't do it in the name of Islam. None of it is required to be a 'good' Muslim. And please let us get our sense of humour and joie de vivre back. Let us stop being boring!

Part Two

VIEW FROM THE GROUND

In the following chapters, a cross-section of Muslims—academics, activists, commentators and students—define the idea of a liberal Muslim, discuss the crisis of liberalism in Indian Islam, and seek to separate fact from fiction in the debate on the Muslim Question.

In a separate interview, distinguished Islamic scholar and former Chairman of the National Commission of Minorities, Dr Tahir Mahmood, expresses his views.

1

ONLY JUDICIARY CAN INITIATE REFORMS

Dr TAHIR MAHMOOD
*Islamic scholar and former Chairman,
National Commission of Minorities.*

Question: *You are a leading voice of reform and have been calling for changes to Muslim family laws for many years now. You must be pretty frustrated at the lack of any progress. What is it that is holding them back? Is it just the mullahs?*
Answer: Yes. I miserably failed to convert the fanatics. I am not 'frustrated' but have given up, realizing that it is an exercise in futility. Muslim masses will never listen to saner voices coming from within the community. They irrationally see their personal law—thanks to the propaganda by the moulvis—as an inalienable

symbol of their religious identity.

To your query, 'what's holding them back,' my answer is: a combination of sickening religiosity, powerful social myths that refuse to die out, a very strong hold of the clergy on the community, religious bigotry, wide-scale legal illiteracy and, above all, the misbelief that moulvis are representatives and spokesmen of God and the Prophet.

Question: *Does the Muslim resistance to reform reflect the wider crisis of liberalism among Indian Muslims? One doesn't hear many liberal voices on this or other issues?*
Answer: Muslim masses naively believe that their personal law in its entirety is written in the Quran and Hadith, and is hence integral to their faith. Those in the community who support reform are generally not learned enough in these fundamental sources of Islam to counter this popular myth.

Though disgusted with the actual practice of personal law, many prefer not to publicly speak about it. They don't want to be seen as an instance of fools rush in where angels (read so-called ulama) fear to tread.

Question: *You've written that it is time for the government to intervene without waiting any more for an initiative from the Muslim community. Given the Muslim sensitivities around the issue, will any government have the courage to act unilaterally? There will be huge Muslim backlash.*
Answer: I know no political dispensation would ever like to antagonize a sizeable section of voters. I have just exposed

the hypocrisy behind their alibi of waiting for an initiative from within the community which they know will never come about—since by 'community' they mean religious leaders and their blind followers only. Those Muslim judges, lawyers and other modern scholars who have been pleading for reform, in the politicians' reckoning, do not represent the community. In these circumstances, no legislative reforms are in sight.

The badly needed reform can come in this country from the judiciary only, though it will be sporadic and piecemeal. In many judgments of the higher courts, Muslim law has already been liberally interpreted in its true spirit. The process needs to be accelerated.

Question: *Why are Indian Muslims so reluctant when Sharia has been reformed in many Islamic countries? Is it because of a lack of liberal leadership?*
Answer: The moulvis believe and propagate that only Saudi Arabia, where the traditional law remains static, is a truly Islamic country—all other Muslim countries which have introduced reforms have gone astray and are under 'Western' influence. Some claim that reforms have been arbitrarily imposed there on unwilling masses, and some have the cheek to dispute if any reforms have really been introduced at all anywhere in the Muslim world.

Question: *What are the specific reforms you would like to see?*
Answer: Three major areas crying for reform are divorce, bigamy, and Wills. Divorce must not be a wholly private affair—the

Quranic requirement of mediation by competent arbitrators should be duly enforced by evolving proper machinery for it.

Bigamy in Indian practice means a man arbitrarily deserting his first wife and bringing in another, which is very different from the Quranic concept of plural wives and hence must be legally prohibited.

Muslims can make a Will of their property only within its one-third portion, and under Sunni schools of law even that is not allowed in favour of would-be legal heirs as identified under the inheritance rules along with their fixed shares—howsoever small the prescribed share of a particular heir may be. Neither of these restrictions is based on any Quranic commandment and hence can be lifted by law.

2

LIBERALLY SPEAKING...

S. IRFAN HABIB
*Historian and formerly Maulana Azad Chair,
National University of Educational Planning and
Administration, New Delhi*

For me, a liberal is one who is not dogmatically committed to his/her religious, cultural or any other identity. Anyone who allows a space for critical thinking. This is true for any liberal in general, and of course for a Muslim liberal as well. Unfortunately, the liberal core within the Indian Muslim community has shrunk over the years. Historically, even during the nineteenth century, we had a large section which could debate and discuss in writing issues related to Islam. It did have detractors then as well, but they were allowed the space to say what they felt like saying. Today that seems to be not so easy.

To your question whether they have let down the community, I don't think so. Their number was always minuscule. I must admit that the Muslim liberal's silence on many issues had always been intriguing to me. The huge difference now is that a large number of erstwhile mute believers have turned vocal and aggressive. The same is true for Hinduism as well. Past decades have seen the peddling of Wahhabi/Saudi version of Islam, with an anti-West rhetoric, which has polarized and empowered many against the 'other'—an imagined enemy of Islam. We need to look for the enemy within, but that sort of voice is not strong enough.

As for the view that one reason for the liberal failure could be that most liberals are left-wing self-proclaimed atheists and therefore don't carry credibility with a deeply religious community, it may be partially true. But even the believing liberals, who were not many but still had a strong presence and acceptability, have now very insignificant numbers.

One major factor is the change in the perception of faith itself. Even the Shia Islam, considered to be moderate till Khomeini happened to it, is now not very different from the Wahhabis, and I do call such Shias as Wahhabi Shias. The liberal Muslim, Left or not Left, does not seem to have any future in India or elsewhere, unless the faith itself takes a liberal or moderate turn.

Indian Muslims did have a strong liberal tradition; the

fanatic Muslims used to be a fringe which is true for other faiths like Hinduism as well. Our Islam in India was culturally composite and I often make a distinction between Indian Islam and Islam elsewhere. That distinction is sadly getting blurred. The Arabization of Islam is homogenizing the heterogenous faith, which I believe is one of the major reasons for the decline of liberal Islam.

3

EVERY DROP CONTRIBUTES TO THE OCEAN

ZEENAT SHAUKAT ALI
*Former Professor of Islamic Studies, St. Xavier's College, Mumbai
Director-General, The Wisdom Foundation*

Although there may be different dimensions to the word liberal, a liberal Muslim would be one who is willing to think about and respect an opinion different from one's own. The vision of Islam is transformation—inclusion in opposition to exclusion; tolerance in opposition to bigotry; open-mindedness in opposition to narrow precincts; advancement in opposition to incarceration. The right of privilege of ideas is the dynamics for such transformation. Liberals are few and far between. But numbers are not the criteria. Every drop contributes to the making of an ocean. Remember

Einstein. It is the silence of Muslim liberals on even moderate reform, leave aside ideas of transformation, that is deafening.

Unfortunately, within the sphere of Islamic jurisprudence, Ijtihad or creative interpretation has been marginalized and even ignored. The egalitarian holistic approach is held hostage to *taqlid* or unquestioning acceptance of authority. Sadly, I know of very few Muslims who have favoured even moderate reform, let aside transformation.

I do believe liberals have let the community down. It is time for them to emerge from their armchair discussions and contribute to civilization. Islamic Liberal discourse needs to play a key role. It is time for them to address Constitutional rights, individual liberty, freedom of thought and expression, the rule of law, accompanied by critical thinking, the ability to transform without fear or favour. This was the role played by Islam in the seventh century. Development, advancement in ideas and progress on national and international affairs are the need of the hour.

There should be no place for intolerance, bias and bigotry.

There have been debilitating factors behind the erosion of liberalism among Indian Muslims. Power politics has played an adverse role throughout the world. We have inherited the situation. Muslims must concentrate and analyze what are the flashpoints of the origins of theological conflict in India. Most conflicts are not faith driven but driven by political opinions to mobilize mass public opinion. When political issues remain unresolved, religion becomes the target. It is important for

Muslims to absorb that fact. The Babri Masjid is today a Title issue, not a religious one. A change of approach will harmonize the long lost tradition of liberalism.

Whether any liberal reforms are likely to take place anytime soon will depend on whether the Muslims permit prudence to prevail. Islam is liberal in essence—it is embracing. It encompasses democracy and secularism that are the bedrock of India's Constitution. Our Constitution is by far one of the best. Education is the key to success—not simply madrasa education but scientific, economic, political and social education. We need to learn from the small but successful and influential Parsi community that it is not merely numbers that make the difference but hard work, clear objectives, liberalism, professionalism and business acumen.

The culture of Islam's munificence, tolerance and liberalism, its culture of nonviolence, conflict transformation, bridge-building and gender justice need discussion. Islam's vision lies in equity and justice—liberals need to explore and concentrate their energies on these aspects. The mindset leaning towards orthodoxy and rigidity needs a metamorphosis if we are to successfully implement constructive reforms.

4

TO HYPHENATE OR NOT IS THE QUESTION

AMIR ALI

Assistant Professor at the Centre for Political Studies, Jawaharlal Nehru University, New Delhi

The liberal-Muslim is an oft-used term in the wider media and comparatively narrower academic discourses. The idea is most likely to be taken recourse to when an atrocity in the name of Islam happens, a terrorist attack for instance, or protests against blasphemous books that can go on to be burned. There follows a clamour to know where the liberal Muslim is and why s/he is not speaking up to condemn the most recent atrocity.

The implications of these anguished enquiries could be many. It could be that there are no liberal-Muslims, the term itself being an oxymoron. It could suggest that there are very few of them, making the need to search for their lost voices a slightly challenging task, approaching the impossible. Or it could mean that they are being held to ransom by the more extremist elements within their ranks, and are being prevented from speaking their liberal minds.

The fundamental problem with the very idea of a liberal Muslim is that s/he would very likely be a 'good Muslim' rather than a 'bad Muslim' in the eyes of liberal establishments, if one were to use the binary offered by political scientist Mahmood Mamdani. In other words, the liberal-Muslim would likely be a figure saying precisely what liberal establishments want. It would almost seem as if liberal establishments have created a template for a good liberal-Muslim. When not many are found, figures from the liberal establishment will then ask in frustrating disbelief, 'Well, why can't you be more like that?' Perhaps the best answer would come from a Black American Muslim, the legendary boxer Muhammad Ali, who famously said: 'I don't have to be what you want me to be.'

Further reinforcing the impossibility of the liberal-Muslim is the fact that any candidate for the category is unlikely to have much credibility amongst the more orthodox elements within Muslims. The liberal-Muslim is likely to be good from the perspective of the mainstream liberal establishment, and bad from the vantage point of those deep within Muslim communities. The impossible liberal-Muslim would then likely be a Janus-faced creature, good on the side facing the liberal establishment and bad on the side facing co-religionists.

To make matters worse, when it comes to the impossibility of the liberal-Muslim, is that the term itself, it may have been noted, is a hyphenated one, a bit like liberal-democracy. The problem with hyphenated terms in which the liberal precedes the hyphen is that it tends to hegemonize, dominate and sometimes even eviscerate the possible potential of the term that comes after the hyphen. A serious case could then be made that the liberal component of the term liberal-Muslim is meant to dilute and thereby contain the Muslim part, making it that much more suspicious in the eyes of many Muslims.

The attempt at being a liberal-Muslim then could be considered akin to a treacherous tight-rope walk, where there is always the danger of being too liberal or not being Muslim enough, and in the process falling on either of the two sides. This dismissal of the idea of liberal-Muslim is not meant to discredit and disparage liberalism per se. There is a clear case for liberal currents to flow through Muslim societies that many Muslims across the world, especially in India will agree, are suffering from a certain sluggish malaise. It was precisely to vigorously rouse them out of this state of slumber that someone like Allama Iqbal wrote the kind of inspiringly frenzied poetry that rejected secularism, nationalism, liberalism and the very tradition of the Western enlightenment itself, from which the previously mentioned gamut of terms have emerged.

The sluggish and despondent malaise that seems to afflict many Muslims in India and across the world is the result of a constant gnawing sense of fear. This is the fear that Islam is somehow in a perpetual state of being endangered in a hostile world. This general grievance is summed up in that one evocative line in Allama Iqbal's *Shikhwa* or Complaint:

Rehmatein hain teri aghyaar ke kaashanon par/ Barq girti hai to bechaare Mussalmanon par

(Forever are your blessings falling on the houses of those who are not Muslims/Forever has lightning been falling on the poor hapless Muslims)

An engagement with liberalism, among many other ideas, is certainly required. This would necessarily come from a set of well-meaning Muslims, who may have a range of ways of relating to what it means to be Muslim. It perhaps should include men and women who may be observant in their religious beliefs, deep believers in Islam, sceptical believers, some who may be not-so observant, and some who may even be agnostic. It would perforce need to include atheists from a Muslim background, sincere in their expression of the fact that they find it difficult to believe in God and Islam. This would, even the most orthodox Muslim may admit, be far better than hypocrisy in religious belief or *munafiqat* as it is referred to.

This engagement with liberalism among other political and philosophical ideas, would then genuinely create the possibility of Muslims comfortable with liberalism, and at the same time their religious beliefs and values. It might be worthwhile to state that this deep and meaningful engagement would still not create a liberal-Muslim in the hyphenated sense of the term.

The only way that I have been able to respond to the question of whether I am a liberal-Muslim, a query often shoved in my face, is to suggest that I am a liberal and a Muslim; and a Muslim and a liberal, in no particular lexical ordering. But I am certainly not a liberal-Muslim. One may add that the engagement with liberalism in the times of Trump et al would be a jihad for not just a Muslim, but anyone opposed to the indecency and loutishness that the Trump phenomenon across the world represents. Jihad certainly does not mean religious war as it is widely and misleadingly understood. It means an intense struggle for justice and the truth.

5

A REASSESSMENT OF THEOLOGY IS THE NEED OF THE HOUR

SULTAN SHAHIN
Founder-Editor of NewAgeIslam.Com
(a progressive Islamic website)

There is no room for liberalism in Islamic theology. Ulema in the Indian sub-continent foam at the mouth, castigating liberalism and its secular, democratic, egalitarian values, while at the same time claiming that Islam is the ultimate source of European Enlightenment. Liberalism is called a manifestation of Dajjal, an evil figure in Islamic eschatology. And yet, Indian Muslims have been fairly tolerant of liberals so far.

What lies behind this paradox and why may it change?

Ideologically, Indian ulema are as fundamentalist and obscurantist as their counterparts in neighbouring Pakistan and Bangladesh. They too consider liberals apostate. Theoretically, apostates are considered deserving of death. But while outspoken liberals are lynched across our borders, not a single liberal Muslim has been killed in India.

Presumably this is because liberal Muslims in India are too few and too ineffective to pose any real problem for the fundamentalists. Indeed, liberals are not even trying to promote their progressive thoughts. Of course, an occasional article appears in an English language newspaper. These are largely inspired by Western liberalism or quote a couple of well-known verses from the Quran, teaching pluralism and co-existence. Too harmless for fundamentalists to bother. They can easily counter that with: Following Western thinkers is like following Satan and the pluralistic, tolerant verses quoted from early Quran were abrogated by the Sword Verses revealed later.

The traditional narrative is that the Quran was a work in progress and instructions in Surah Taubah that were revealed a few months before Prophet Mohammad passed away, constitute the final message. They call for disavowal of all contracts with pagans and even People of the Book, now that Muslims were victorious, and abrogate all those instructions of peace and co-existence that were taught earlier in Makkah when Muslims were a persecuted minority. So, despite an occasional liberal intervention, the theology is safe and Muslim fundamentalists can continue to teach that Islam stands for world domination and the complete elimination of idol-worship from all parts of the world.

Another reason why fundamentalists tolerate liberal Muslims is that it is the latter who have the intellectual wherewithal to fight for what is called the Muslim Cause. Like minorities elsewhere, Indian Muslims too face discrimination at various levels. And it is liberal Muslims who struggle to get them justice. So, when an organization like Muslims for Secular Democracy is formed, the fundamentalist recognizes that even if some of its members may be liberal and thus 'apostates' deserving the punishment of death, they have an impeccable record of fighting for justice for the Muslim community. While the concept of Human Rights or Secular Democracy is anathema to the Muslim fundamentalists, in India, they have no option but to fall back on the liberal values of the Indian Constitution for their own protection. Thus, we saw the curious spectacle of Jamaat-e-Islami, the most fundamentalist of all Muslim organizations, organizing a Forum for Secular Democracy in the company of secular Hindu intellectuals during the Emergency in 1975. Now, the Jamaat also runs a political party swearing by the liberal values of the Indian Constitution, though according to its founder Maulana Syed Abul A'la Maududi's ideology, they should not even vote in India.

We never find Muslim fundamentalists speaking for the rights of religious minorities in Pakistan or Bangladesh, but they think Indian Muslim minorities deserve freedom of religion and expression. Not surprising, therefore, that they tolerate Indian Muslim liberals and interact with their liberal Hindu friends too.

These liberals are needed for the protection of human rights for the Muslim community.

The crisis of Indian Islam emanates primarily from its theology. There is a consensus of all schools of thought that Islam has to dominate the world; non-Muslims may be allowed to live in, but not rule any country. If at all our ulema disagree with the likes of self-declared Khalifa Baghdadi, it is only in terms of tactics and timing. Initially, the declaration of Islamic State was welcomed; one celebrated scholar even wrote to Baghdadi, addressing him as *Ameerul Momineen*, leader of all Muslims. It was only when the so-called Islamic State started broadcasting its brutalities that the chorus in its support died down.

However, the ulema do not present their theology in public as it actually is. They are ever ready to proclaim Islam as a religion of peace. That is why when an educated Muslim youth turns to religion, he is horrified to find how hypocritical Muslim society is. He discovers that the only theologically approved relationship between a Muslim and a non-Muslim is that of the ruler and the ruled. The moment people turn to religion, they get the same message from all the learned scholars. From Imam Ghazali to Imam Taimiya, Sheikh Sirhindi to Shah Waliullah, Hassan al- Banna to Maulana Maududi, the consensus is: Muslims should go out on offensive Jihad at least once a year; Muslim rule should keep expanding year after year till Islam finally conquers the world.

Muslims swear by this theology, teach this theology to their children in madrasas but make no effort to follow it. The Islamic textbooks taught in the Saudi Kingdom teach that Muslims should have no relationship with Jews and Christians, and yet the Kingdom enjoys the best of relations with the West. No wonder, the majority of youths joining the so-called Islamic State were Saudi. The one thing that the youth today hates, is hypocrisy. This can be seen across continents, resulting in the rise of Right wing everywhere. Violent Islamic extremism too is thus more a revolt of the younger generation against the hypocrisy of the older generation.

As more of our youth turn to religion and easily educate themselves online in Islamic theology of consensus, they discover that the 'apostasy' of liberals is the biggest of crimes in the eyes of God and has to be punished in this very world.

The first thing the first Rightly Guided Caliph Abu Bakr had done after assuming power was to fight what is called Ridda (anti-apostasy) wars against those who had left Islam following the death of the Prophet. Muslims who follow the Salaf (first three generations of Islam) should follow this example. Normally this is the job of a Muslim State. But since present-day Muslim States are slaves of Taghut (Satan or even earthly tyrannical powers), so the radical argument goes, Muslim groups or individuals can take it upon themselves to punish the apostate.

That the Quran does not prescribe any punishment for apostasy or blasphemy is of no concern of our ulema. Even if a Muslim with religious education points this out, he is branded a liberal and apostate. A traditionalist cleric of the stature of Maulana Waheeduddin Khan, a preacher of peace and pluralism, has to live under police protection. In the absence of a coherent and internally consistent counter-narrative, Indian Muslims will not be able forever to remain immune to the wave of radicalization and violent extremism sweeping across the Muslim world.

We Muslims have to decide if we want to live honourably in the twenty-first-century world of complex and close interactions among all social groups. The world in which one could conquer territories and occupy it legitimately died almost a century ago. The Kellogg–Briand Pact of 1928, later refined in the UN Charter signed on 26 June 1945, has created a different world. Most Muslim countries are signatories to the Charter. Empires can no longer be built or expanded indefinitely by conquest of new territories as before. The Islamic theology of violence, exclusivism and world domination has no place in this modern world. Muslims need to urgently evolve a new theology of peace, pluralism and gender justice suitable for this new world. We need a coherent and sincere counter-narrative which does not rely on hypocrisy to sustain peaceful relationships with our neighbours.

This is not very difficult. One doesn't have to be a liberal to discover in Islam all the principles needed to live honourably in the new age. It is only a matter of correct interpretation, keeping the context in mind and as the Quran has asked us to do in numerous places, finding the best meaning of words used in verses of the Quran.

Accepting one basic principle alone can change much of the traditional narrative. Instructions are given in every war that become irrelevant the moment that war is over. Prophet Mohammad had to fight wars for the very survival of Islam

1400 years ago. These wars were fought in the desert of Arabia in conditions vastly different from the situation today. The directions given in those wars can no longer be applicable to Muslims in the contemporary world. This is plain common sense. The moment fundamentalists accept these minimum demands of rationality, much of the crisis in Islamic theology can be resolved. To say that these temporary war-time orders, the so-called Sword Verses, have abrogated the foundational, constitutive verses of the Quran, revealed when the actual religion was being revealed in Makkah, is nothing short of being blasphemous.

We can make a beginning by at least starting to debate these issues in a rational manner. If the theologians of the first few centuries of Islam made a mistake in creating a violent narrative of Islam, we don't have to continue to follow them blindly. Numerous verses of the Quran exhort Muslims to think, to reflect, to reason. Muslim fundamentalists would do well to start pondering the antiquated nature of their medieval theology in the light of contemporary issues. The poet-philosopher of Islam, Allama Mohammad Iqbal had called for a reconstruction of Islamic religious thought almost a century ago. It is time we heed him at least now.

6

BRING MULTIPLICITY AND PLURALITY BACK

IRFANULLAH FAROOQI
Assistant Professor, Sociology,
South Asian University, New Delhi

'Bhaiyya daadhi thodi choti kar dein? Sahi rahega. In dinon thodi choti theek hai' (Should I trim your beard a little? It will be better. These days it is better to keep it short.) These were the words uttered by the hairdresser who I had gone to for a haircut. This was a shop in a South Delhi Muslim locality, Jamia Nagar (mostly referred to as a ghetto.) Uttered with an unsettling normalcy, these words have remained with me not just as words but a commentary from the nooks of crass everyday existence.

The hairdresser's concern regarding the length of my beard is not to be located in the commonsensical frame of appearance. It is to be situated outside the grammar of style and trend. It was not my first meeting with him. As a matter of fact, he could say what he said because of a degree of comfort created by our regular meetings. His words hinted at the problems with appearance of an undesirable nature. Beard of a certain length contributed to that appearance. It was therefore better (read safe) to seek recourse to an informed and strategic invisibility. Perhaps he wanted to say something to the effect of liberal/illiberal binary. While he could not frame his views the academic way, the sheer wisdom of it could not be overlooked. The rootedness of his concern accounts for why those words of his have remained with me ever since.

Raised in a typical Muslim locality, my upbringing was a blend of various experiences. My father, an academic trained in an Islamic seminary, would always get a water-gun and balloons on the occasion of Holi and firecrackers on Diwali. Sunday mornings were about recitation of the Quran and watching the popular serial Ramayana on TV, one following the other. I distinctly remember going to watch the traditional burning of Ravana's effigy with my parents. Alongside these extraordinary experiences of connectedness, the essentials of a religious upbringing were never lacking in my family.

I became acquainted with the term 'liberal Muslim' only during my university years. Before that, a Muslim was a Muslim. I had a disconcertingly naïve understanding of the community and its overall structure. It is in the university that I was asked by some of my friends if I was a practising Muslim, to which

I could not answer. In my world, Muslims were joined together by a shared belief in oneness of the Almighty and, therefore, non-practising Muslims were not outside its fold. It is only after a reasonable familiarity with the roots of the question, that I could understand how my response was needed to serve the world of sharp operational definitions. The inquiry perhaps was not as much in relation to knowledge as it was with respect to subjection to a world of constructs. I did not fit that well in the otherwise efficient world of definitions, and my cluelessness vis-à-vis the query perhaps hinted at the shallowness of the question itself.

It is not easy to come up with a comprehensive response to what it means to be a liberal Muslim in India. With respect to a community that is subjected to stigmatization, alienation, demonization and what not, any perceptive student of life and society cannot miss out on what disturbingly simplistic divisions such as liberal/illiberal, moderate/radical, progressive/conservative and so forth, can do.

Rather than the definition, I am more inclined towards understanding what gets acknowledged as a liberal practice or sentiment in the community by those located within the community and those standing outside. Within the community a liberal is someone who gives concession every time there is an apparent conflict between essentials of Islam and demands of life in an exceedingly modern world. She would be someone invoking, more often than not, the uncommonly compatible aspect of Islam. In circles outside the Muslim community, a liberal Muslim is one who engages with the modern world fully and identifies herself more strongly with something other than religion. In a way it is about Liberalism *in* Islam in the case of the former, and Liberalism *and* Islam with respect to the latter.

A frightened community is bound to doubt its plurality. It finds scope in closures. For us, then, the job is to bring multiplicity and plurality back to the centre-stage. In that connection, liberal Muslim to me is someone who firstly engages with diversity within the Muslim community, and subsequently demonstrates an open-mindedness towards plurality of religious expressions in the society. She is someone who is able to think above sects, see beyond forms, and is always holding on to the dynamic, evolving, and non-procedural character of everything that falls within the human world. For instance, various jurisprudential sects of Islam have specified ideal timespans for the compulsory five prayers to be said in a day. However, on many occasions we have seen that people switch to another sect as per the demands of day to day life. In my own family, on several occasions, we have prayed before the prescribed *Hanafi*[*] timespan and followed the *Ahle Hadith*[**] sect (one that is absolutely antithetical to the *Hanafi* sect.) This informed crossing of boundaries can only be understood by looking at how, for an informed believer, it is the primacy of performing the duty rather than the *way* in which it is to be performed.

---

[*] A dominant jurisprudential sect in North India.
[**] A sect that projects itself against jurisprudential sects in general and *Hanafi* sect in particular.

To me, it is important to approach the idea of a liberal Muslim from this perspective, for it questions the manner in which a liberal Muslim is defined in terms of her outlook and take on things that mostly fall outside the Muslim community. This perspective pushes us towards the Islam and Liberalism argument (Islam and liberalism as two distinct territories) wherein politically charged discourse around freedom of expression, dissent, tolerance, human rights, reason, individualism, and rule of law is constructed at the drop of a hat. When a liberal Muslim is defined and, even better, understood primarily in terms of intra-community transactions, the politics that facilitates fragmentation of everyday lived reality falls flat.

Notwithstanding the caution on our part in underlining the essence of the idea of a liberal Muslim, we cannot neglect the ways in which the construct offers little scope for those who are religious. Much worse is the condition of those whose looks and attire foreclose even the slightest possibility of any conversation or exchange. The sheer violence implicit in denying a person a conversational space cannot be overstated. From within the community too, given Muslims' preference for recognition rather than identification, traditions, customs and religious practices are approached with a strategic scepticism. As the progressive lot within the community indulges in declaring the 'acceptable levels of Muslim-ness,' numerous recommendations are made in relation to making Islam more compatible with the modern secular world. They blame the traditional lot of the community for doing nothing with respect to preparing the community in terms of critical self-introspection. Many of these indulgent liberals from the community express concern over not 'looking like a Muslim,' without thinking even once that a Muslim-looking person is not given the privilege to express her concern over not being seen as a liberal.

As someone who sees remarkable potential in the society-religion interface, I am quite interested in the purpose served by liberal Muslim as a construct with respect to bashing the hardliners and conservatives of Muslim community.

As we get swayed by the sheer charm of pitting moderate liberals against radical conservatives, we leave behind a world of clichéd frames of reference that has no scope whatsoever of expanding our horizon of understanding. In my own family, where do I put my mother who did not go to college, is a devout believer, and, alongside, contributed immensely in letting her children fully engage with the atrociously secular and uncommonly liberal world of universities? How do I define my brother—a *Hafiz** and an academic—who lives in accordance with Islam and at the same time reads literature classics and watches first-rate world cinema?

It turns out then that there is a pressing need to come around an understanding of a liberal believer who expresses herself through a much deeper association with religion.

At a time when religion-based violence has become rampant, it is obligatory on our part to reclaim the religious. I say this

---

*A person who has memorized the whole of Quran.

because with my supposedly religious looks, I do not want to be denied a conversation. My face should not rest my case. As a Muslim with a liberal outlook, I genuinely believe in my freedom to carry a Muslim-ness that refuses to be assessed by shallow standards of compatibility with modernity. I do not want my ability to think and question to be limited to my response to ISIS, Talibans, cartoon controversy, executions in the middle-east, homosexuality and so forth.

Lastly, perhaps we need to ask ourselves what is it we are more inclined towards in the term liberal Muslim: liberal or Muslim. The sequencing itself is somewhat suggestive in that respect. It commands a certain kind of religiosity. We must not pay heed to that command and celebrate the sheer complexity everything acquires the moment it is touched by the human. Robert Browning asked us to develop interest on the dangerous edge of things. Let the liberal Muslim offer that possibility to us.

7

OPENNESS IS THE KEY

FAIZUR RAHMAN
Islamic researcher and founder,
Islamic Forum for the Promotion of Moderate Thought

In my view, a liberal Muslim is one who is open to not just other interpretations of Islam but also other religious views as well. He or she is not someone who praises liberal Western leaders such as Jacinda Ardern for the exemplary solidarity with Muslims, yet does not utter even a whimper of protest when Christians, Hindus, or Muslims belonging to other sects are persecuted in Muslim countries. A liberal Muslim is a practitioner of human values found in the Quran and the teachings of Prophet Mohammad rather than an attention-seeking exhibitionist of piety.

Unfortunately, there aren't many liberal Muslims of this kind today.

As for your question whether liberal Muslims have let down the community, there are hardly any liberal Muslims today to 'let down the community.' Those who have let down the community are the pseudo-liberals whose idea of liberalism is to combine the skullcap and a Western suit, or the niqab and accented English, yet speak the language of medieval obscurantism that emphasizes personal religiosity over egalitarian humanism.

As to whether one reason for the liberal failure could be that most liberals are left-wing self-proclaimed atheists and therefore don't carry credibility with a deeply religious community—any atheist or agnostic person criticizing religious believers, be they Hindus, Muslims or Christians, will be treated as an 'outsider' and not taken seriously. The problem with most atheist liberals is that they wear their atheism on their sleeves and are as preachy as sectarian clerics.

Also, the believers are put off by the display of excessive left-wing rationalism which is projected as the *only* cure for all ills facing a religious community. I know of Muslim 'liberals' who think that Muslims would progress only when they start questioning the authorship of their holy book, the Quran. These over-enthusiastic 'reformers' rely on the outdated views of medieval commentators to conclude that the Quran is far from the human rights or gender equality document that Muslim apologists make it out to be.

This is akin to Islamophobes asserting the correctness of the ISIS understanding of Islam to demonize Muslims.

Certainly, the Muslim community will not take them seriously.

8

THE CLOSED DOOR OF IJTIHAD NEEDS TO BE OPENED

MUSHTAQ UL HAQ AHMAD SIKANDER
Human rights activist and commentator on Muslim issues, Srinagar

Liberal Muslims—the term sounds like an oxymoron both to Muslims and non-Muslims.

For Muslims, a liberal or liberated Muslim means a Muslim who has given up practising Islam and its tenets, and does not bother much about either what is considered lawful or the forbidden, in Islam. Technically, they continue to be Muslim but their opinion about Islam and Muslims is not acceptable to the community despite being valid.

For non-Muslims, a liberal Muslim is one who does not

demand reservation, dines with them but does not inhabit the Muslim ghettos, and never decries the discrimination against Muslims in India.

So, liberal Muslim is on their own with little support from the wider community and even from society in general. The Muslim ulama and community do not consider them Muslim enough to be trusted, while non-Muslims accuse them of not being liberal enough. So liberal Muslims are always decried and labelled as stooges of the West by their own community, while for others, they remain 'communal' Muslims. These fault lines have never been negotiated or redrawn.

With the advent of colonialism, the Muslim community responded to the socio-political and educational system of the colonizers through three broad reactions. First there were those who were for the wholesome adoption and imitation of the Western colonial model. Then, there were those completely hostile and opposed to the model. The third category was of those who accepted the model with exceptions and tried to incorporate changes in it to make it compatible with Islam. So, there was a division between traditional and liberal Muslims.

The divide continues in free India too. The madrasas are giving birth to a traditional, backward-looking leadership while the secular education is shaping a different leadership. The division is complete and compartmentalized. Each section respects the tacit contract of not breaching the territory of the other.

Madrasa-educated ulama with sectarian outlook always express opinions about Islam, even if these are sectarian, and hold sway over the masses. Whenever they find their position and status threatened, they initiate a movement decrying 'Islam is in danger.' They threaten the liberal opinionated Muslim with fatwas and community boycott. The political parties of all hues need these madrasa-trained mullahs, moulvis and ulama for consolidating the Muslim vote bank as they can influence the opinion of voters. This group certainly needs to be appeased as their power cannot be underestimated. Plus, over the centuries they have adorned, developed and evolved a certain type of dress code including beards, coupled with the reinforcement of that image by media, in such a way that even Muslims cannot accept anyone as an Islamic scholar or community leader if he does not possess these features. So liberal Muslims lose out here as well, since they do not possess these features. The community cannot and will not recognize them as leaders.

A liberal Muslim is one who believes in the principle of *sulh-i-kul* (peace with all), upholds the fact that his is not the only source of truth but that there are various versions of truth in different ideologies, religions and viewpoints. A liberal Muslim, even if she does not observe the rituals of Islam, implements and practises its universal values like egalitarianism, social justice, charity, supporting the destitute and contributing to activities aiming at the empowerment of the downtrodden. A liberal Muslim is tolerant when it comes to the interpretation of Islam, forging unity both intra and inter-faith. A liberal Muslim is a crusader for the cause of women's rights, empowerment through education, and democracy. Liberal Muslims uphold the postulates of no-violence. Unlike traditional ulama, they do not indulge in mudslinging, false allegations and issuing of legal decrees.

The door of Ijtihad, or debate, that has been closed by the traditional ulama needs to be opened up. Only liberal Muslims have the courage to undertake the same. They should prepare themselves for this job and it will take some time to develop the requisite expertise among the liberal Muslims who can then indulge in Ijtihad. The traditional ulama have created a false aura around themselves that they are the epitome and zenith of piety, with huge followings, and when they do not dare to undertake Ijtihad, how can liberal Muslims who are in a minority, do so? But as the times and necessity demands Ijtihad, despite their opposition, the Ijtihad will be acceptable to the community if undertaken by liberal Muslims.

Being a liberal Muslim brings with it a plethora of accusations and allegations meant to browbeat the liberal Muslims. They are routinely dubbed as Western stooges, working at the behest of the West and trying to Westernize Islam. The West and its ideologies have been the most misunderstood by the Islamic Revivalists. When the ulama do not have a logical or Islamic answer to an interpretation of Islam that is different from theirs, the simple escapist route is to label it 'Western.' However, the reality is that the West is most happy with the traditional ulama as it helps reinforce the Islamophobic and violent image of Islam.

The fact is that liberal Muslims have no love lost for the West and its policies. The West has been successful in exploiting and using traditional ulama and their interpretation of Islam for its own imperialistic goals—whether it be the balkanization of USSR or in undermining the Arab Spring.

Western powers patronize autocratic, authoritarian and sectarian regimes like Saudi Arabia at the cost of the denial of basic human rights and liberal values such as freedom of speech, right to form associations and rule of law.

The lack of liberal Muslim leadership is because most of them are afraid or in awe of the traditional ulama. They shy away from advocating a new interpretation of Islam for fear of a backlash from the community and ulama. Most of them suppress their inner call and lack the courage to stand up for their liberal values. Political parties too do not want to associate with liberal Muslims for fear of losing traditional Muslim votes. Thus the liberal Muslims who are articulate and opinionated are marginalized even by the secular political parties.

Liberal Muslims have their work cut out in bridging the divide between the traditional ulama and themselves, and initiate a dialogue. They need to become role models by demonstrating a strong commitment to values that can inspire the masses and motivate them to follow the liberals.

But are they up to it?

9

ISLAM HAS BEEN HIJACKED BY EXTREMISTS

SYED OMAIR AHMED
Describes himself as a 'religious person'

Islam means 'to surrender' or submission. So, what does it require us to surrender? It is basically man's ego that is responsible for creating all evil, and this is required to be understood and dissolved or 'surrendered.'

Allah gave the human race the ability to think, reason, and make rational decisions. Islam addressed the natural intelligence of men, and a small community that accepted its teachings began practising Islam—bringing about a deep, fundamental and revolutionary transformation in a backward tribal society. The first thousand years witnessed a spectacular rise and popularity of Islam. Drawn by its ideas of egalitarianism, compassion and equality, people from around the world rushed to embrace it.

But then like all successful projects, it became a victim of its own success as complacency set in, and vested interests took over with conservatives clamping down on independent thinking in the name of 'pure' Islam. While Islam retreated, the predominantly Christian West embarked on a path of industrial and technological revolution, not to mention a cultural renaissance. Meanwhile, the Islamic world became infested with factions and sects plunging it into a spiral of internal sectarian battles. Even today, the Muslim world is torn apart by ceaseless self-destructive conflicts—all in the name of Islam. People are fighting and destroying each other, bringing untold miseries unto humankind. And justifying it in the name of Islam—and Allah.

Islam has been hijacked by extremists who have no mindspace for individual freedom, free speech or reasoning. These self-styled guardians of 'pure' Islam, bankrolled by leading Islamic powers, want to drag Islam back to medieval times by misinterpreting or—more dangerous—selectively interpreting Sharia to justify their tactics. They have reduced Islam to violent jihad, and suicide bombings—and their followers to robotic puppets. Islam has become a wasteland of ideas and new thinking. The Muslim mind has been induced to close itself against the modern world for fear of being 'infected' with ideas that they claim would undermine Muslim identity. And, alas, Indian Muslims are no exception.

But hopefully 'spring' will come soon. The near future will see Muslims return to the original spirit of Islam and its values of egalitarianism, tolerance and equality. Right now it may seem like a distant dream because liberalism has not risen the way it should have, and things might get worse before they turn for the better.

CONCLUSION

THE WAY FORWARD

There are two broad narratives or rather counter-narratives about Indian Muslims.

In one, advanced by Muslims themselves, we see them as an exuberantly diverse lot buzzing with liberal voices that the outside world pretends not to hear for political reasons.

In the other, propagated by their detractors, they are presented as a monolithic and intolerant community swarming with religious fanatics.

Reading these extreme narratives, you wouldn't think they are talking about the same people. This shows the extent to which the debate around Muslims or the so-called Muslim Question has become polarized. But let us stick to the facts.

And the stark fact is that even after making allowances for historical factors such as the impact of Partition and the discrimination and prejudice they face in their daily lives, Muslims cannot shrug off the responsibility for being perceived as they are by their detractors.

The image of an insular and inward-looking community has a basis, and the community has contributed to it with its prickly cultural and religious sensitivities. A tendency to see everything through a Muslim or Islamic prism has led to the shrinking of a secular viewpoint. An issue must have a bearing either on Muslims or on Islam to motivate them; a liberal or secular cause in itself is not good enough for them to get involved, as I have shown in previous chapters.

Increasingly, I detect a level of illiberalism that surprises me. A strain of illiberalism has always existed in the community (as it does in all communities) but over the years it has grown instead of abating. Even educated middleclass Muslims have not been able to escape its effect, however much they might protest. The difficulty of defining a liberal Muslim says it all. There are of course some high-profile Left liberal Muslims but most don't even identify as practising Muslims (some are openly atheist) and their aggressive liberalism alienates even the moderates in the community.

Partly out of arrogance and partly naïveté, they have taken on the role of great reformers without even making any attempt to engage with the community. This is typical of their crass

CONCLUSION

approach and it has nearly done as much damage to the cause of Muslim liberalism as the mullahs. Their brassy rejection of Sharia and a tendency to classify anyone who disagrees with them—which means pretty much every practising Muslim—as a fundamentalist, has made ordinary Muslims, including reform-minded moderates, suspicious of the liberals. And liberalism itself has come to be seen as a threat to Muslim identity.

But here is another thing. This illustrates the depth of the liberal leadership vacuum among Muslims that a cabal of self-proclaimed atheists—regarded by the mainstream community as beyond the pale—has become its liberal public face.

Have we then reached a dead-end in selling liberal reforms to Muslims? No, not really. For all the apparent doom and gloom and the perception that the community has developed a bunker mentality, there is still a lot to play for—provided we play it right. Five years ago I wrote a book, *India's Muslim Spring: Why Is Nobody Talking About It?* focusing on a new generation of practising moderate Muslims who were trying to drive change in the community's outlook. With their comparatively more forward looking and liberal outlook, these young men and women—I argued—were potential harbingers of an Indian 'Muslim spring.'

Since then, the public discourse under the Narendra Modi government has turned virulently anti-Muslim, and this has led to a hardening of the Muslim mood across the community, including among its moderates. I had warned at the time that 'it could still go all belly-up if the new mood in the Muslim community is not matched by a change in...anti-Muslim prejudice.'

Which, unfortunately, is what has happened.

And here is another cause for concern: If right-wing Hindu nationalists are allowed to carry on their hate campaign unchecked, it is safe to say goodbye to any hope of a Muslim spring for good. None of this, however, detracts from my contention that any change will come from within the community itself and the potential agents of change are already there in the form of a new crop of young moderate Muslims who don't see any conflict between religiosity and modernity so long as modernity doesn't mean throwing out the baby with the bathtub. Sharia is important to them but they acknowledge it does require tweaking to bring it in the modern age. They believe in incremental reform, starting with practices that, to begin with, are of doubtful provenance—triple talaq, polygamy, status of women—and those that affect Muslims adversely in their daily lives. Their approach is more in tune with the mindset of a deeply conservative community than the Left liberals' advocacy of overnight root-and-branch reform. But most importantly, the former are community insiders in a manner of speaking, and carry credibility with their people. Something Left liberal outsiders don't.

Indian Muslims' liberal dilemma is part of a larger crisis of liberalism in global Islam with the rise of Saudi-inspired Wahhabi Islam based on a literal and often misleading interpretation of the Quran. There is also the fact that Islam is inherently prescriptive and not compatible with the Western Enlightenment ideas of liberalism and secularism.

Secularizing Islam will need a revolution but meanwhile we

can focus on gradual reforms aimed at opening up debate and free speech at least within India. There are specific areas where it is possible to bring about change without waiting for the secular revolution—such as raising the status of Muslim women by reforming family laws around inheritance, property rights, and divorce; promoting a softer interpretation of the Quran and a progressive understanding of Islam; grooming a new generation of educated forward-looking imams; and teaching Quran in local languages.

Tunisia is a good example of a liberal Muslim-majority country. Its official religion is Islam, it is governed by an Islamist party (Ennahdha Party inspired by Egypt's Muslim Brotherhood and the Iranian Revolution), and its legal system draws on Sharia but it bears no resemblance to other Islamic countries in the Muslim world. It has the most progressive laws on women's rights and freedom. Practices like polygamy and men unilaterally divorcing their wives, are banned. There are no Sharia courts.

Under a Code of Personal Status, regarded as the most modern civil code in North Africa and the Muslim world, women enjoy full legal status and, unlike in other Muslim States, there are no restrictions on what they can and cannot do. Women have full freedom to own and run businesses, take part in political activities and run for Parliament. In 2017, Tunisia became the first Arab country to declare domestic violence against women a criminal offence. It also abolished the law allowing rapists to escape punishment by marrying the victim. Tunisia's political system—a republic with an elected Parliament—is rated as the only fully functioning democracy in the Arab world.

The Tunisian experience shows that while trying to secularize Islam may be a fool's errand, it is possible to marry Islam with modern values of liberalism and social justice. It must be pointed out, however, that the current process of liberalization started back in the 1950s under Habib Bourguiba after Tunisia won independence from France. Still it is significant that it has not only continued under an Islamist party but gained further momentum.

So, yes, 'We can,' given the will. And, importantly, provided we do it the right way—not try to impose it from above but do it in consultation with the community, and do it slowly. This, essentially, is what many Western Muslim dissidents are calling for—not a secular revolution, but 'an attempt to modify, adapt and reinterpret Islamic practice to make religious discourse more human,' as Ayaan Hirsi Ali points out in his book *Heretic: Why Islam Needs A Reformation Now*. Indeed, she believes that a process of reformation is already underway. Which is saying a lot—coming from someone who carries a heavy baggage of alleged anti-Islamic prejudice and is hated by many Muslims worldwide.

The best evidence that a Muslim Reformation is actually underway,

> 'is the growing number of active dissidents and reformers around the world.[...]These individuals are not clerics, but informed citizens speaking out on the basis of reason and conscience. They are urging either a fundamental reinterpretation of Islam or a change in the core doctrines

CONCLUSION

of Islam. Some of them have left the faith, seeking reform from the outside, whereas others seek to reform Islam from within. Their arguments focus on the importance of viewing the Qur'an and the Hadith in a historical context and on respecting man-made civil laws as legitimate, overriding Sharia religious law.

(*Heretic: Why Islam Needs A Reformation Now*, Ayaan Hirsi Ali)

In India also, there are a number of 'informed' Muslims seeking a similar path to reform. The way to help them is to dial down on threats to impose reforms from above. Such talk is seen as bullying the community into submission, and further hardens attitudes, alienating even those who might otherwise be in favour of changes. Muslims, including moderates, are sensitive about any attempt to interfere with the Muslim Personal Law—a favourite target of both Left liberals and the Hindu right. The right approach will be to start a dialogue with the community aimed at winning its trust and allaying its fears. The important thing is to create a climate in which Muslims begin to see themselves as partners in change rather than as targets of hostile forces out to undermine their religious and cultural identity.

Indian Muslims have a long, often forgotten history of moderation, and with the right approach the old spirit can still be revived. The precondition is that both Left liberal Muslims and right-wing Hindu nationalists need to keep their hands off.

POSTSCRIPT

HOW THEY DID IT

The patronizing Left liberal view that a practising and devout Muslim cannot be a liberal reformer is repudiated by the history of Muslim reforms in India, mostly brought about by those derided for their beards and skullcaps. Here are a few random examples of prominent nineteenth and twentieth century Indian Muslim reformers who were also devout Muslims and earned the sobriquet Maulana—a Muslim revered for his religious learning or piety. They saw no contradiction between religiosity and modernity—and led by personal example to prove it.

SIR SYED AHMAD KHAN (1817-1898)

On 17 October 2017, the two-hundredth birth anniversary of Sir Syed Ahmad Khan, founder of Aligarh Muslim University, was celebrated with much fanfare in and around Aligarh University and its illustrious alumni. In the post-1857 era, which saw the decline of Mughal empire and rise of British power all over India, Sir Syed Ahmad Khan was a modernist in pre-modern India.

He was born in a well-known Delhi family on 17 October 1817. A government employee, an Islamic scholar, journalist, and educationist he has left behind a huge collection of articles, books, etc. He was a *munsif* by profession, who also used his writing for advocating social reforms. On social and religious issues, he ran a magazine, *Tahzebul Akhlaq* (Social Reformer.) Sir Syed wrote in its first edition (1870):

'The objective of issuing this journal is to persuade Indian Muslims to adopt a complete degree of civilization meaning culture, so that the hatred with which the civilized (cultured) nations view them should go away and they may also be said to be exalted and cultured nations of the world. Civilization is an English word which we have translated as culture but its meaning is very vast. It means to raise all the intentional actions, morals and matters and society and civilization and its ways, and the use of time and knowledge and every kind of arts and skill to a high quality of finesse, and to deal with them with great excellence and method, which is the source of real happiness and bodily quality and from which dignity and grace and value

POSTSCRIPT

and stature is attained and the difference between barbarity and humanity is witnessed...' (*Dabistan-e-Tarikh-e-Urdu* by Hamid Hasan Qadri, Karachi, 1966)* Although at that point of time, culture and civilizations could be used interchangeably, but what he is saying here is still relevant.

Sir Syed advocated the process of dialogue and discussion on religious matters. He also wrote *The Mohamedan Commentary on the Holy Bible* for better understanding between the Christians and the Muslims. His famous work '*Asar-us-Sanadid*,' founded the tradition of Indian archaeology.

In the post-1857 era, he encouraged Muslims to empower themselves by acquiring education. Sir Syed Ahmad Khan preached modern education, but not by any compromise on the commandments of Quran and Sunnah.

Primarily an educational venture, Sir Syed's greatest achievement was his Aligarh Movement. In 1867, Sir Syed started the Muhammadan Anglo-Oriental (M.A.O) School when he was posted at Aligarh. In 1869-70, he studied the British educational system during his visit to England. Following the pattern of British boarding schools, he decided to make M.A.O. High School a boarding. The School later became a college in 1875. Sir Syed established his college on the model of Oxford and Cambridge. His solution for the problems of the community was modern education. In 1920, the Muhammadan Anglo Oriental College, became Aligarh Muslim University. His purpose was to build

---

*Quoted in https://cafedissensus.com/2017/11/04/sir-syed-ahmad-khan-1817-1898-a-modern-muslim-in-a-pre-modern-age/

a college following the modern British education system but without compromising its Islamic values for the empowerment of the poor and backward Muslim community.

Sir Syed wanted this College to act as a bridge between the traditional and the modern, the East and the West. Dr Sir Mohammad Iqbal observes: 'The real greatness of Sir Syed consists in the fact that he was the first Indian Muslim who felt the need of a fresh orientation of Islam and worked for it—his sensitive nature was the first to react to modern age.'

Maulana Altaf Hussain Hali, Sir Syed's ardent disciple who wrote *Hayat-e-Javaid*, biography of Sir Syed Ahmad Khan, wrote about the regressive attitude of Muslim notables in the nineteenth century. Many Muslim religious scholars organized a full-fledged front against the teaching of modern education. Some Nationalists criticized him for being pro-British.

Sir Syed's modern vision for the community is still a guiding force for Muslims of the subcontinent. He paved the way for many thinkers to emerge later like Iqbal, Deputy Nazeer Ahmad, Maulana Azad, Altaf Hussain Hali. The historical role played by Sir Syed and his Aligarh Movement cannot be overlooked while discussing post-1857 era of Indian history and socio-political reforms in the Muslim community.

MAULANA ABUL KALAM AZAD (1888-1958)

Abul Kalam Ghulam Muhiyuddin, born in Mecca, Saudi Arabia, on 11 November 1888, who was respectfully known as Maulana

POSTSCRIPT

Abul Kalam Azad, was a venerated freedom fighter, journalist, politician and educationist. His father was an Indian, while his mother was an Arab and the family moved to Calcutta (Kolkata) when Azad was just two years old.

Still in his teenage years, Abul Kalam Azad acquired a high reputation for his writings on religion and literature in the regular Urdu journals of the time. Teachings of Sir Syed Ahmad Khan influenced Azad. Along with learning English, he went on a quest to read about Western philosophy, history and contemporary politics, travelling to Afghanistan, Egypt, Iraq, Syria and Turkey. A scholar of languages like Persian, Arabic, Urdu, Bengali, Hindi, his commentaries on religion and philosophy, exhibited his knowledge. Azad compiled many treatises interpreting the Quran, the Hadith, and the principles of Fiqh and Kalam or theology. He started weeklies like *Al-Hilal* (The Crescent) in 1912 in which he challenged traditional interpretations of the Quran and also opposed British policies; it was banned by the British in 1914. In 1915, he started *Al-Balagh* which continued till 1916. His other publications included *India Wins Freedom, Ghubar-e-Khatir, Tazkirah, Tarjumanul Quran*, etc.

He was a prominent leader of the Khilafat movement, close to both Gandhiji and Pandit Nehru. He became the youngest president of the Indian National Congress in 1923 and was again elected as president in 1940. Azad often faced imprisonment for participating in the Freedom Movement with other nationalist leaders. He rejected the theories of communal separatism advocated by the All India Muslim League and Jinnah. He was also a strong advocate of harmony, unity and education as a means to empower citizens.

The first education minister of Independent India, Maulana Azad had a keen interest in politics, history, languages and held the firm view that education would show the path to the nation's development.

All India Council for Technical Education (AICTE), Sahitya Akademi and many more institutions were founded by him. In 1953, he was instrumental in setting up the University Grants Commission (UGC) and the first Indian Institute of Technology (IIT.)

'A very brave and gallant gentleman, a finished product of the culture that, in these days, pertains to few,' was how Jawaharlal Nehru had described Azad. In 1992, he was conferred the Bharat Ratna posthumously.

'Full eleven centuries have passed by since then. Islam has now as great a claim on the soil of India as Hinduism. If Hinduism has been the religion of the people here for several thousands of years, Islam also has been their religion for a thousand years.

'Just as a Hindu can say with pride that he is an Indian and follows Hinduism, so also we can say with equal pride that we are Indians and follow Islam. I shall enlarge this orbit still further. The Indian Christian is equally entitled to say with pride that he is an Indian and is following a religion of India, namely Christianity.'

(*From the Presidential Address—Maulana Abul Kalam Azad*, I.N.C. Session, 1940, Ramgarh)

POSTSCRIPT

MAULANA MOHAMMAD ALI JAUHAR (1878-1931)

Maulana Mohammad Ali Jauhar, also known as Mohammad Ali, was born in 1878 in Rampur to a wealthy and enlightened family of Pathans of Yousaf Zai clan of the Rohilla tribe. Shaukat Ali and Zulfiqar Ali were his other famous brothers, also known as Ali Brothers. Although his father died early, his wise and spirited mother Abadi Bano Begum, enabled him and his brothers to get good education. They were sent to the Muhammadan Anglo-Oriental college, Aligarh. Mohammad Ali showed exceptional brilliance throughout his college career and stood first in the B.A. examination of the Allahabad University. Later in 1898, Mohammad Ali went to Lincoln College, Oxford, for further studies where he got an Honors degree in Modern History and devoted himself more to the study of history of Islam.

After his return to India, he joined as education director for the Rampur state, and later for almost a decade served in the Baroda civil service. He wrote articles for various newspapers like *The Times*, *The Observer* and *The Manchester Guardian* and other Indian newspapers, in both English and Urdu.

He started his first newspaper *Comrade* in English in 1911, but was banned in 1914 for publishing an article 'Choice of Turks' in 1913. In 1924, publication was resumed with great difficulty but again discontinued in 1926. In 1913, his Urdu newspaper *Hamdard* started and was quite popular too. But publication of anti-British articles resulted in frequent imprisonment of its editor. His two brief collections of Urdu poetry and prose have been published titled *Kalam-e-Jauhar*.

He had the unique distinction of having headed Indian National Congress and Muslim League at different points in his life. In 1906, Maulana Mohammad Ali Jauhar started his political career as a member of Muslim League. He was unanimously elected as President of Muslim League in 1917, while he was still in detention. He joined Indian National Congress in 1919 and became its National President in 1923 for a brief period. He was a staunch supporter of freedom movement and a leading light of the Khilafat Movement. He led a delegation to London for Khilafat movement in 1920. On his return from England, he established Jamia Millia Islamia in 1920 at Aligarh, which was later shifted to Delhi.

He challenged the Western powers over the issues of Palestine and Turkey (over the fate of Sultan vis-á-vis nationalist Mustafa Kemal.) When he died of a stroke on 4 January 1931, the Mufti Amin ul Husseini of Palestine gave him the honour of a final resting place in Jerusalem near Masjid e Aqsa.

He understood well the relationship of State and religion and famously wrote:

> Where God commands I am a Muslim first, a Muslim second, and a Muslim last, and nothing but a Muslim… But where India is concerned, where India's freedom is concerned, I am an Indian first, an Indian second, an Indian last, and nothing but an Indian.

MAULANA HASRAT MOHANI (1878-1951)

Maulana Hasrat Mohani or Syed Fazl-ul-Hasan was born in 1878 in a small town, Mohan, in UP. His ancestors had migrated from Nishapur, Iran. Mohani was a brilliant student in his high school days and later took admission in M.A.O. College, Aligarh (Aligarh Muslim University.)

He later started his own journal *Urdu-i Mualla* from Lucknow and newspaper *Mustaqil* from Kanpur. He was recognized as a talented poet. His books are *Kulliyat-e-Hasrat Mohani* (Collection of Hasrat Mohani's Poetry), *Sharh-e-Kalam-e-Ghalib* (Explanation of Ghalib's Poetry), *Nukaat-e-Sukhan* (Important Aspects of Poetry), *Mushahidaat-e-Zindaan* (Observations in Prison), etc.

In 1921, it was Mohani who coined the immortal slogan of Indian Revolution: 'Inqilaab Zindabad.' In 1921, at the Ahmedabad session of the Indian National Congress, with Swami Kumaranand, and in the presence of Ramprasad Bismil and Ashfaqullah Khan, Hasrat Mohani was the first person to demand 'Complete Independence' or 'Poorna Swaraj' for India. On 25 December 1925, he chaired the reception committee of the first Indian Communist conference. He was also a member of the drafting committee of Indian Constitution led by Dr B.R. Ambedkar, with whom he disagreed on many aspects and did not sign the final draft as Member of the Committee.

Russian Revolution had a huge impact on Mohani. He became active in communist politics and later became part of Communist Party of India (CPI.) After he was expelled from the CPI for unknown reasons, in 1931 Mohani formed his own party 'Azad Party,' whose main aim was to work for a federal form of government against unitary form, a principle which remained central to his politics. Mohani identified with the communist philosophy and tried to interpret it in the light of concepts of Islam in order to bring the Muslim population closer to it. In an Urdu couplet, he identified himself as a Sufi and a Muslim communist.

'My way is the sainthood and revolution; I am a Sufi, momin (faithful) and Communist Muslim.'

Although he was associated with Muslim League from its inception (only in 1936 it became active), he did not favour the 'two nation theory' of Mohammed Ali Jinnah. After Partition, when many League members decided to go to Pakistan, Mohani remained in India. He was a strong advocate of Hindu-Muslim unity and was also known as the 'Maulana who loved Krishna' as he wrote verses celebrating Krishna and also was a regular visitor to Mathura during Janmashtami. He was a religious practising Muslim, went for Hajj (pilgrimage to Mecca, Saudi Arabia) several times and led a simple life. He never accepted government allowances or stayed at official residences. Instead, he stayed in mosques and used to go to the Parliament in a shared tonga.

Rakhshanda Jalil* writes 'seeing no duality between his assiduous roza-namaaz and ardent krishn bhakti, this bearded,

---

*https://sabrangindia.in/article/how-indian-freedom-fighter-and-urdu-poet-expressed-his-love-krishna

POSTSCRIPT

shervani-clad gentleman from Mohan in the Unnao district of western Uttar Pradesh, resorts to the more rustic Awadhi to express his grand passion:

Mann tose preet lagai Kanhai
Kahu aur kisurati ab kaahe ko aayi
Gokula dhundh Brindaban dhundho
Barsane lag ghoom ke aayi
Tan man dhan sab waar ke 'Hasrat'
Mathura nagar chali dhuni ramaye

My heart has fallen for you, Kanhai
How can it think of anyone else now?
I searched for him in Gokul and in Brindavan
I even went till Barsana looking for him
Having sacrificed everything for him, I, Hasrat
Am now going to set up my abode in Mathura

Locked up in the Yervada Central Jail in Poona for his 'seditious' activities, with the coming of Janamashthami he cannot contain his longing to go to Mathura:

Mathura ka nagar hai aashiqui ka
Dam bharti hai arzu issi ka
Har zarra-e sar-zamin-e Gokul
Daara hai jamaal-e dilbari ka
Barsana-o Nand Gaon mein bhi
Dekh aayein hain jalwa ham kisi ka
Paigham-e hayaat-e jaavidaan thha

Har nagma-e Krishn bansuri ka
Voh noor siyah ya ki 'Hasrat'
Sar-chashma farogh-e-aagahi ka

Mathura is the city of love
All my desires are centred on it
Every particle of the dust of Gokul
Possesses loveliness and comeliness
Even in Barsana and Nand Gaon
I have seen that certain someone's splendour
Whose message of reality is eternal
As is every note from Krishna's flute
Like a dark radiance or is it Hasrat
Like a spring of water gushing knowledge.

DR. ZAKIR HUSAIN (1897-1969)

Born on 8 February, 1897, in Hyderabad, he was the country's first Muslim President, from 13 May, 1967, until his death on 3 May, 1969. He belonged to a Pathan upper middleclass family, who later settled at Qaunganj in the district of Farrukhabad, Uttar Pradesh. His father, Fida Husain Khan, was a very successful lawyer, but died when Zakir was only ten years old.

Zakir Husain went for higher education to Mohammadan Anglo-Oriental College (now Aligarh Muslim University.) Only 23 years of age and a student of the MA class, he was among the small group of students and teachers who decided

POSTSCRIPT

to establish a National Muslim University by the name of Jamia Millia Islamia. In the 1920s, Zakir Husain's quest for knowledge also took him to Germany where he received a Doctorate from the University of Berlin in Economics. He acquired a deep love for European art and literature, and music during his three year stay there.

Being the co-founder of Jamia Millia Islamia, he also served as its Vice-Chancellor from 1927 for twenty-one years. Under Dr Zakir Husain, Jamia became closely associated with the Indian freedom movement.

Dr Zakir Husain was appointed Vice-Chancellor of the Aligarh Muslim University, in November 1948 in the post-Partition era. It was a difficult time in the history of the University as many teachers and students had left for Pakistan. He guided Aligarh Muslim University through those tumultuous years till 1956. He was also nominated as member of the Indian Universities Commission. He became the Chairman of the Indian National Committee and the World University Service, and in 1954 he was elected as the World President of the organization. From 1956 to 1958, he represented India on the Executive Board of the UNESCO. He was also nominated to the Rajya Sabha. After serving as the Vice-President for a term of five years, Dr Zakir Husain was elected President of India on 13 May, 1967. He remained the Chairman, Central Board of Secondary Education, till 1957, a member of the University Grants Commission till 1957, a member of the University Education Commission in 1948-49 and of the Educational Reorganisation

Committee of Bihar, Uttar Pradesh and Madhya Pradesh. He had also served as Governor of Bihar from 1957 to 1962 and as Vice-President of India from 1962 to 1967. He was awarded Padma Vibhushan in 1954 and in 1963 he was awarded the Bharat Ratna, India's highest civilian honour. He was awarded D.Litt. (Honoris Causa) by the Universities of Delhi, Calcutta, Aligarh, Allahabad and Cairo. In his deeply moving inaugural speech he said that the whole of India was his home and all its people were his family.

Dr Zakir Husain had translated Plato's *Republic* into Urdu and also helped in bringing out an anthology on Ghalib when he was in Germany.

A nationalist follower of Gandhian tradition, Dr Husain believed in upholding the highest moral values and lived up to them, believing in principles of democracy with individual freedom and self discipline.

First President to die in office on 3 May, 1969, he is buried in the campus of Jamia Millia Islamia, New Delhi.

REFERENCES

https://cafedissensus.com/2017/11/04/sir-syed-ahmad-khan-1817-1898-a-modern-muslim-in-a-pre-modern-age/ accessed on 20 April, 2019
https://www.amu.ac.in/ourfounder.jsp accessed on 20 April, 2019
https://www.thebetterindia.com/164143/iit-education-freedom-fighter-maulana-abul-kalam-azad/ accessed on 21 April, 2019
https://www.inc.in/en/leadership/past-party-president/abul-

kalam-azad accessed on 21 April, 2019
https://www.culturalindia.net/leaders/maulana-abul-kalam-azad.html accessed on 20 April, 2019
http://jauharuniversity.edu.in/mohammad_ali_jauhar.html accessed on 22 April, 2019
https://www.dawn.com/news/1154854 accessed on 22 April, 2019
https://www.newsclick.in/hasrat-mohani-remembering-freedom-fighter-communist-and-muslim accessed on 22 April, 2019
https://sabrangindia.in/article/how-indian-freedom-fighter-and-urdu-poet-expressed-his-love-krishna accessed on 22 April, 2019
http://www.gloriousindia.com/biographies/dr_zakir_husain.html accessed on 22 April, 2019
https://en.wikipedia.org/wiki/Zakir_Husain_(politician) accessed on 22 April, 2019)

APPENDIX 1

IN THE WORDS OF A PRACTISING MUSLIM WOMAN

URUJ*

I studied in a non-Muslim school, of which I have good memories. I got unconditional love there. After my 10th standard I was sent to a Muslim school, where I got close to my religion. I started wearing hijab and I never faced any issue related to that. The class had all kinds of students from different cultures and different religions. After that I started looking for opportunities for further studies. I was turned down by several colleges because I wore hijab. It was my first brush with anti-Muslim prejudice. I still remember that traumatic day when I was not able to question

---

Post-graduate scholar, Jamia Millia Islamia, Delhi

their action or answer anything about my identity.

A Muslim woman faces a lot of upsetting situations and is stigmatized for all sorts of irrational reasons. People question your identity, your hijab, your belief and customs. When you decline to shake hands with a man, people consider you narrow-minded, but for me it is a part of my belief—rightly or wrongly. When a Muslim succeeds, people forget which culture, custom and belief he or she belongs. We have a good example of A.P.J Abdul Kalam. Before he became famous, he was identified as a Muslim, but when he became successful people overlooked his Muslim identity.

I always think why my mother becomes anxious when I'm not at home. Why I feel anxious when I reach any security checkpoint. It is because of the prevailing Islamophobia. Recently during a competitive exam, they asked me to remove my hijab as per the security requirements. This time I challenged them and I explained about my identity. And when I did this, others came forward to support me. So, everyone is not an Islamophobe. India is full of humane and peace-loving people. India's strength lies in its diversity.

APPENDIX 2

STRAIGHT TALK*

IRSHAD MANJI

Believers: Conduct yourself with justice and bear true witness, even if it be against yourselves, your parents, or your kin.' (Quran, 4:135)

I have to be honest with you. Islam is on very thin ice with me. I'm hanging on by my fingernails, in anxiety over what's coming next from the self-appointed ambassadors of Allah.

When I consider all the fatwas being hurled by the brain trust

---

*Reproduced from the Special Indian Edition of Irshad Manji's 'The Trouble With Islam Today: A Wake-Up Call for Honesty and Change' published by imprintOne in 2005. It was published in arrangement with Random House, a division of Random House of Canada Limited. It is being reproduced with the permission of imprintOne. Copyright rests with Irshad Manji

of our faith I feel utter disappointment. Don't you?

I hear from a Saudi friend that his country's religious police arrest women for wearing red on Valentine's Day, and I think, since when does a merciful God outlaw joy—or fun? I read about victims of being stoned for 'adultery,' and I wonder how a critical mass of us can stay stone silent.

When non-Muslims beg us to speak up, I hear you gripe that we shouldn't have to explain the behaviour of other Muslims. Yet when we're misunderstood we fail to see it is precisely because we haven't given people a reason to think differently about us. On top of that, when I speak publicly about our failings, the very Muslims who detect stereotyping at every turn then stereotype me as a sellout. A sellout to what? To moral clarity? To common decency? To civilization?

Yes, I'm blunt. You're just going to have to get used to it. In this letter, I'm asking questions from which we can no longer hide. Why are we all being held hostage by what's happening between the Palestinians and the Israelis? What's with the stubborn streak of anti-semitism in Islam? Who is the real colonizer of Muslims—America or Arabia? Why are we squandering the talents of women, fully half of God's creation?

How can we be so sure that homosexuals deserve ostracism— or death—when the Quran states that everything God created is 'excellent'? Of course, the Quran states more than that, but what's our excuse for reading the Quran literally when it is so contradictory and ambiguous? ...if we don't speak out against the imperialists within Islam, these guys will walk away with the show.

And their path leads to a deadend of more vitriol, more violence, more poverty, more exclusion. Is this the justice we seek for the world that God has leased to us? If it is not, then why don't more of us say so publicly?

Through our screaming self-pity and our conspicuous silences, we Muslims are conspiring against ourselves. We're in crisis, and we're dragging the rest of the world with us. If ever there was a moment for an Islamic reformation, it is now.

You may wonder who I am to talk to you this way. I am a Muslim Refusenik. That doesn't mean I refuse to be a Muslim; it simply means I refuse to join an army of automatons in the name of Allah...

You'll want to assure me that what I am describing isn't 'true' Islam. I hope you're right. That is why I'm writing this open letter—because I believe that we Muslims are capable of being more thoughtful and humane than most of our clerics give us credit for. But for the sake of an honest discussion, I have to challenge you to come clean about the Islam that you reflexively defend. Is this Islam in its real form or Islam as an ideal?

The United States Constitution guarantees liberty and justice for all, as an ideal. Muslims know that the reality is very different. As people of conscience, we have to address Islam's realities too.

I think Prophet Mohammad would have embraced this distinction between the real and the ideal. When he was asked to define religion, he reportedly replied that religion is the way we conduct ourselves toward others. A fine definition—simple without being simplistic. And yet, by that definition, how we

Muslims behave, not in theory, but in actuality is Islam. Which means our complacency is Islam. It also means the power is ours to restore Islam's better angels: those who care about the human rights of women and minorities.

To do that, though, we have to snap out of our denial. By insisting that there is nothing the matter with Islam today, we're sweeping the reality of our religion under the rug of Islam as an ideal, thereby absolving ourselves of responsibility for our fellow human beings, including our fellow Muslims. See why I'm struggling.

By writing this open letter, I'm not implying that other religions are problem-free. Hardly. The difference is, libraries abound with books about the Trouble with Christianity. There is no shortage of books about the trouble with Judaism. We Muslims have a lot of catching up to do in the dissent department.

Whose permission are we waiting for?

APPENDIX 3

LISTEN TO SANER VOICES ON MUSLIM LAW REFORM*

TAHIR MAHMOOD

'It is a sensitive matter, initiative must come from the community'—since my student days political leaders have been using this alibi for not reforming Muslim law. Which section of Muslims do they expect to come forward with an initiative? When Hindu law was reformed and codified in 1955-56 rulers of the day had faced resistance from religious circles but they were firm about leading the community out of its ancient legal traditions. When the Christian divorce law of 1869 was liberalized by Parliament

---

*Published in the Hindustan Times on 6 May 2016. Original version published in Finger on the Pulse: Socio-Legal Concerns of 1998-2018, Tahir Mahmood, Satyam Law International, 2019. Reproduced with author's permission.

in 1991, was the proposal not opposed by church leaders? Why, then, this special treatment for the Muslims? Have there been no saner voices already among them advocating necessary reforms?

In 1970 eminent jurist Asaf Ali Asghar Fyzee had published his monograph *Reform of Muslim Personal Law in India*, suggesting measures for necessary changes in the professedly divine law on polygamy and divorce, ending with the remark:

'Where the human conscience is moved by rank injustice it is for us to find a solution and to bring our law into line with every other system of jurisprudence, giving justice to those to whom it is denied.'

In 1972 former Chief Justice of India Mohammad Hidayatullah concluded his Introduction to D.F Mulla's book *Principles of Mahomedan Law* with this thought-provoking observation:

'If the injunctions of the Quran and Hadith are not lost sight of, it is possible to make changes by legislation in a widening area. The lead is coming from the Muslim countries and it is to be hoped that in the course of time the same measures will be introduced in India also.'

In my various books on Muslim law published since 1972, I have been explaining authentic Muslim law, pointing out its distortions by influx of time, explaining how the true Quraanic law has been restored by legislation in the Muslim countries and pleading for similar reforms in India. In my two journals— the *Islamic and Comparative Law Quarterly* launched in 1981 and the *Religion and Law Review* started in 1992, I have published numerous articles, mine and of others, exposing the un-Islamic

APPENDIX 3

nature of Muslim law in practice and prompting the rulers to initiate proper remedial measures. The Shah Bano judgment of the Supreme Court (1985) cited from one of these periodicals my 'appeal to the Muslim community to display by their conduct a correct understanding of Islamic concepts on marriage and divorce.'

When Muslim religious circles demanded supersession of the Shah Bano ruling by legislation and the government seemed to be favourably disposed to it, former Chief Justice Hameedullah Beg [then chairing the Minorities Commission] had so advised the rulers, suo motu:

'Although we may make some compromises with mulla-led Muslims yet we have to try to lead them out of darkness into light and not allow them to lead us into darkness.'

(Minorities Commission, Annual Report 1985-86)

When a Bill was drafted by the Muslim Personal Board for the enforcement of the traditional Muslim law on divorced women's maintenance as per its own understanding, I was invited by the Board President late Abul Hasan Ali Nadwi to give my opinion on it. My note opposing it due to its repugnance to true Islamic law, not accepted by him, was sent to the government—yet the Board's draft-bill was accepted and passed in a hurry. Late Asghar Ali Engineer spent a lifetime in pressing for necessary legislative reform to ensure justice to those deprived of it in the name of a sacred law. His Bombay-based Centre for the Study of Secularism and Society and its mouthpiece, the *Indian Journal of Secularism*, has been awakening the Muslims to the need for necessary reforms in their law in tune with the Quranic teachings,

Women have not been lagging behind. There is a long list—from Lucknow's Begum Qudsia Aizaz Rasool of the 1960s to Sadia Dehlavi of our times, pressing for social reform to free Muslim women from the shackles of the Indo-Anglican misinterpretation of Islamic law. The Lucknow-based Muslim Women's Personal Law Board and the Mumbai-based Muslim Mahila Andolan have been highlighting the plight of victims of a distorted view of Muslim law and demanding legislative action.

In the Sarla Mudgal case of 1995, finding that under the shelter of Islamic law on bigamy as popularly misunderstood, married non-Muslims were indulging in it after sham conversion to Islam, the Supreme Court applied brakes on the fraudulent practice. Justice RM Sahai in his separate judgment spoke of the need to codify Muslim law and advised the government 'to entrust the responsibility to Law Commission which may in consultation with Minorities Commission examine the matter and bring about the comprehensive legislation in keeping with modern-day concept of human rights for women.'

Next year in 1996, on taking over as the Chairman of National Minorities Commission, I reminded the government of the learned judge's advice, to no avail. During 2007-09 as a Member of the Law Commission of India I wrote a number of reports recommending measures for necessary reforms in respect of marriage registration, polygamy by sham conversion, problems with civil marriages and the outdated Shariat Act of 1937.

Two important matters concerning Muslim law are currently

APPENDIX 3

before the Supreme Court—a PIL on gender discrimination in Muslims law registered suo motu, and Shayera Bano's case challenging Constitutional validity of triple talaq. A large number of Muslim men and women, old and young, have supported favourable decisions by the court.

Do these sane voices in favour of reforms in Muslim law made year after year not qualify to be taken as 'initiatives from the community'? What are the custodians of State authority waiting for?

Who do they expect to come forward asking for reform—the Deoband seminary, or the Muslim Personal Law Board? If so, the Muslims will have to remain content with their outdated personal law till the Day of Judgment.

APPENDIX 4

BEYOND MULLAHS AND MARXISTS*

HASAN SUROOR

A Hindu friend once told me, even as he profusely apologised for his bluntness, that there was only one kind of Muslim—the fundamentalist kind. The idea of a 'liberal' Muslim was a 'misnomer' according to him. Such a person was first and foremost a liberal who happened to be a Muslim because of the sheer accident of having been born in a Muslim family.

'Their liberalism doesn't derive from Islam. It has nothing to do with their being Muslims. They are liberals despite being Muslims and not because they are Muslims. I have yet to meet

---

*Reproduced from 'India's Muslim Spring: Why Is Nobody Talking About It?' published by Rupa Publications, 2014;—courtesy Rupa

APPENDIX 4

a devout Muslim who doesn't have fundamentalist views. And mind you, I'm 70 plus and have known at least three generations of Muslims,' he said.

The notion that a practicing Muslim cannot be liberal has become conventional wisdom.

And, to be honest, I have often found myself in agreement with this view. Working in Delhi as a journalist until the late 1990s, I had a hard time finding sane, liberal voices, even in educated Muslim circles, on issues such as free speech, Muslim personal law, women's rights, and secularism. There were either the agnostic/atheist, mostly, left-wing secular Muslims who felt almost embarrassed to be defined by their religious identity, or there were 'mainstream' devout Muslims—defensive, insular, intolerant and deeply suspicious of their secular peers, contemptuously dismissing them either as communists or government stooges.

There is no doubt that all faith groups are divided along liberal/fundamentalist lines (Hindus, Sikhs and Christians have their own share of fundamentalist 'mullahs') but the divide among Muslims was particularly stark. It was as if these were not two sections of the same community but two separate communities with parallel and irreconcilable worldviews.

During my travels (for this book) I found young Muslims vigorously debating the challenges facing India's 170-million strong Muslim community and what it should do to haul itself out of the hole it is in. What particularly struck me was their courage to acknowledge what previous generations had doggedly refused to—namely, the community's own role in its destruction. For the first time there is a willingness to face up to the fact that many of the wounds the Muslims suffered, and for which they blamed others, were actually self-inflicted. 'Suicidal' is how young Muslims describe the tactics of successive post-partition generations. They believe they have been handed a legacy that speaks of their elders' profound failure to produce an enlightened and credible leadership. And they are angry.

'Muslims are architects of their own misery,' said Aamir Shahzad, a religiously post-graduate history student of Lucknow University with barely suppressed fury. 'I hate to say it but my fathera and grandfather's generations have failed us. Their priorities have been wrong and we are paying for their mistakes. They allowed mullahs to become our spokesmen. And look where we are today.'

As an illustration of wrong priorities, many cite the fight that the community picked up over Babri Masjid. 'I am not that it was not an important issue but if we had made the same sort of noise over discrimination that Muslims face in everyday life, and in demanding good education and jobs, it would have made more sense,' argued Meraj Haider who runs a successful real estate business in central U.P...The community I was told must get out of its siege mentality; stop seeing enemies everywhere and start on a new slate. There is a deep generational divide, especially in the 18-25 age group. They believe that their parents' generation had been too 'defensive' about its Muslim identity and, for all its secularism, tended to see India essentially as a 'Hindu'

APPENDIX 4

country and Muslims as a persecuted minority. Its perception of its Muslim identity was 'too negative,' according to them.

I have some sympathy with this view though the theory, especially in the academia, that Muslims have always suffered from a deep existential 'identity crisis' as to who they were —'Muslims first or Indians first' (an agonized on this has raged for as long as I can remember) is vastly exaggerated… The identity issue has its roots in Partition. Not many Muslims will acknowledge this but let us be honest: it is a myth that every Muslim who stayed back in India was prompted by a sense of nationalism or was against the idea of Pakistan. Many stayed back simply because they found the sheer logistics of migration too daunting; others held back of the fear taking the plunge into an unknown and uncertain future; some tested the waters and decided it was safer to hang back; and, indeed, quite a few–including some progressive Muslims—actually moved to Pakistan and returned when they discovered that it was not the promised land it was cracked up to be.

So, the post-partition generation struggled with a massive historical baggage that, among other things, made it deeply conscious of its identity and of its place in a Hindu-majority India—an 'infection' that it passed on to successive generations. Muslims from that generation admit to suffering a 'Muslim complex' as some put it. But they attribute it to the political climate of the time.

'We were a product of our time. There was a climate of suspicion of Muslims because of Partition, and so on. There were communal riots now and then, Urdu was being crushed because they said it was the language of Muslims…it was not easy to forget you were a Muslim,' said Ahmed Qadri, who ran a library of Urdu books and journals in Old Delhi in the 1960s. He was forced to close down the library as Urdu publications and their readers declined, leaving him with few books to lend and even fewer customers to lend to.

'What happened to me happened because I was a Muslim… so could I not be conscious of being a Muslim?' he asked.

Muslims of his generation say that the Hindu Right made it impossible for them to forget their minority status. They were regarded as 'lower orders who should know their place.'

For the younger generation of Muslims, on the other hand, Partition has no special resonance. It is something they read about in history books and feel no need to 'obsess about,' as one young Muslim woman put it. Nor do they feel any special affinity towards Pakistan, which, if anything, they regard as a failed state—and an embarrassment.

All this makes them less conflicted about their identity and minority status. They see themselves as any other Indian citizen except that they happen to be Muslims. They argue that Muslims are not the only minority group in India and there is no reason why they should put themselves in a special box.

But here is the paradox. Precisely because they don't suffer from the sort of identity crisis their parents did, they feel less inhibited about flaunting their 'Muslim-ness.' That explains the proliferation of beards and hijabs, and the rush to the masjid, a growing global trend among young Muslims. But they insists that this assertion of their 'Islamic identity' does not diminish their Indian-ness, which is what ultimately defines them. Allama Iqbal wrote, 'Hindi hai hum watan hain, Hindustan hamara.' And that pretty much sums up the modern Indian Muslim. Damn the beard.

APPENDIX 5

ISLAM AND ITS INTERPRETATIONS*

HASAN SUROOR

WHAT IS ISLAM?

I know Islam's critics will be dying to answer this question, but it is more important to hear it from Muslims themselves because, after all, it is their conflicting interpretations of Islam which are behind so much of the confusion and mayhem around the world. A religion of peace, yet a religion which is invoked to wreak such mindless violence. A religion which is said to accord dignity, respect and equality to women; yet a religion in which a woman's

---

*This article first appeared in The Hindu on 23 September, 2014

APPENDIX 5

testimony is only half as good as a man's. A religion which exhorts its followers to gain knowledge even if it means 'going to China'; yet some of whose most noisy campaigners despise knowledge and are prepared to kill little girls for attending school. And a religion which preaches tolerance and coexistence; yet which has become synonymous with hate and intolerance.

So, what is Islam really about?

ISLAMIC THEOLOGY

In his book, *What Is History?* E.H. Carr urged people to read the historian before they read his or her history in order to get a sense of where that historian is coming from. Many Muslims will say that the same analogy applies to Islam: its interpretation depends on who is interpreting it. So, extremists will interpret it to suit their own agenda while moderate Muslims would offer a different interpretation. But the trouble with this explanation is that it is at odds with the claim that Islam is so perfect, that it is beyond debate or interpretation. Its teachings and edicts are meant to be immutable. Take it or leave it. This claim itself then takes a knock when we hear so many bewilderingly different interpretations that, let alone non-Muslims, even ordinary Muslims are left confused and frustrated. A healthy internal debate is one thing, but tawdry public disputes over the fundamentals of Islam— jihad, sharia, caliphate—is quite another.

What, then, is the problem?

To be fair, it is not entirely the fault of interpreters, and in this I include those who wilfully misinterpret it to promote their sectarian or extremist ideas. The potential for misinterpretation and misunderstanding lies in Islamic theology itself. The Koranic text is a minefield of ambiguity, allowing people to cherry-pick its equivocal and often contradictory verses to back their argument. Similarly, it is easy to manipulate Hadith (a compilation of Prophet Mohammad's sayings and teachings), another major source of legitimacy for Islamic acts. This is because they are too numerous, were pronounced in vastly different situations, and compiled many years after his death with the result that their precise meaning was frequently lost in translation. Sometimes they were quoted outside the original context. They are routinely plucked out of context to support bizarre claims Then there is the problem of 'inauthentic' Hadith—sayings attributed to the Prophet which he may or may not have uttered. Even many authentic Hadith have been found to be flawed because of misinterpretation or contextual errors.

ON JIHAD

We have seen a great deal of quibbling over the meaning of jihad. Muslims insist that the 'real' concept of jihad does not involve violence and bears no resemblance to Islamists' interpretation of it. The 'real' or 'greater' jihad, they say, means a peaceful inner spiritual struggle. An armed struggle against an external enemy is regarded as 'lesser' jihad and permitted only in specific circumstances—for example, in self-defence. Theoretically true.

Yet, it is also true that around the dining table in Muslim households, the term jihad is invariably used in its violent sense and mentioned in the same breath as 'kaafirs.' I grew up in an extremely liberal environment, but I don't recall, in private conversations, jihad ever being referred to in its philosophical sense. In Indian Muslim discourse, the term normally used for personal struggles, whether social, economic or emotional, is 'jaddo jehad' derived from Urdu.

Extremists can be accused of inventing circumstances that, in their opinion, would justify violent jihad, or of targeting the wrong 'enemy,' and using appallingly brutal methods of executing their 'jihad.' But they cannot be accused of inventing the notion of violent jihad itself. There is no denying the streak of violence which—according to distinguished British Pakistani Islamic scholar Ziauddin Sardar—is 'inherent' in Islam. But that is not the point. All religions, especially those which set out to gain followers through proselytisation and to conquer empires, have violent histories. Campaigns to 'Christianise' Pagan Europe in the Middle Ages were not always peaceful, and then, of course, there is the bloody history of Inquisition and the Crusades.

To a large extent, Islam is often wrongly and wilfully portrayed as being somehow unique in having had a violent history. But what is unique about Islam is that while other religious movements, particularly Christianity, got over their early violent origins, it failed to move on and update its theological precepts. There has been no Islamic equivalent of Enlightenment and Renaissance, and the Islamic mindset remains awkwardly out of step with historical progress, and therefore with modern times—a hiatus reinforced by attempts to assert an Islamic identity through beards and hijabs.

But to return to the question, 'what is Islam?' ask any Muslim and they will solemnly enumerate all its nobler aspects: its emphasis on community and oneness which has made it the world's fastest growing religion; its rejection of caste or class; the spirit of inquiry it fosters; its command not to bow to any temporal authority (thumbs down for authoritarianism and dictatorship); its stress on simple and spartan living; a unique system of zakat to prevent concentration of wealth in a few individual hands; a complete 'no, no' to social and economic exploitation; and its egalitarianism. Prophet Mohammad personally oversaw huge reforms in the pre-Islamic slavery practices in Arabia and appointed a former Ethiopian slave, Bilal Ibn Ribah as the first Muezzin in Islam after helping him gain freedom.

FACES OF ISLAM

Muslims will cite Koranic verses and Hadith to underline Islamic injunctions against violence; its command to treat women with respect and accord them equality; its message of tolerance, love, brotherhood, and its exhortation that we treat even our enemies with respect and try to win them over through love and persuasion rather than force. But this is one face of Islam. It also has another, less pleasant, face. For, the Islam preached by the Taliban and their fellow travellers is also Islam; and if you ask

APPENDIX 5

them, they will also cite Koranic verses and Hadith to back their claims. Their methods may be extreme but their philosophy does derive legitimately from the same Islamic theology that the good face of Islam does. Muslims must stop being in denial about it.

And this brings us back to what lies at the heart of the problem with Islam—namely the somewhat rough-and-ready nature of the fundamentals of Islamic sources, including the Koran, the central religious text of Islam comprising truths which, Muslims believe, were revealed to the Prophet by Allah from time to time until his death. The Koranic text, in the form of 'aayts' (verses), is not thematically linked nor provides context with the result that an 'aayt' which might have originated in a specific context is sometimes contradicted by another 'aayt' on the subject but stated in a different context. This allows a free-for-all scramble for people to grab what might suit them in a given situation. Hence the confusion and the spectacle of extremists and their opponents both quoting the Koran in support of their positions. There is a similar confusion over Hadith, as explained earlier.

The way out is for an Islamic equivalent of the New Testament. Learned Islamic scholars need to put their heads together and present basic scriptures in a manner that the meaning and context of every 'aayt' and every Hadith is made unambiguously clear, leaving no room for misinterpretation or misrepresentation. This annotated text should then be declared as the authorized version of Islamic beliefs. Otherwise, we will continue to struggle to understand what real Islam is while leaving the field open for fanatics to distort it at will.

RECOMMENDED READING

An Introduction to Islam
David Waines
Cambridge University Press

A World Without Islam
Graham E.Fuller
Hatchette India

Concise History of Sunnis and Shi'is
John McHugo
Speaking Tiger

Heretic: Why Islam Needs a Reformation Now
Ayaan Hirsi Ali
Harper,

Ideals and Realities of Islam
Syed Hossein Nasr
The Islamic Texts Society, Cambridge, UK

Islam Without Extremes: A Muslim Case for Liberty
Mustafa Akyol
W.W. Norton & Company

India's Muslim Spring: Why Is Nobody Talking About It?
Hasan Suroor
Rupa

Moderate or Militant: Images of India's Muslims
Mushirul Hasan
Oxford University Press

Making Sense of Pakistan
Farzana Shaikh
C. Hurst & Co

No God But God: The Origins, Evolution and Future Of Islam
Reza Aslan
Random House

Rethinking Islam in the Contemporary World
Carl W. Ernst,
Edinburgh University Press

RECOMMENDED READING

Standing Alone in Mecca: A Pilgrimage into the Heart of Islam
Asra Q Nomani
HarperCollins India

Stranger to History: A Son's Journey through Islamic Lands
Aatish Taseer
Picador

The Crisis of Islam: Holy War and Unholy Terror
Bernard Lewis
Weidenfeld & Nicolson

The House of Islam: A Global History
Ed Husain
Bloomsbury

The Trouble with Islam Today
Irshad Manji
ImprintOne (Special Indian edition)

ACKNOWLEDGEMENTS

When I imagined this book, I didn't realize how sensitive the subject was to many Muslims, and more crucially I discovered there were too many gaps in my grasp of the many twists and turns in the history of Islam.

Luckily, I was able to get help from some of the best minds in the field, and I owe a big debt of gratitude to them—particularly, Dr Uzma Azhar for her invaluable inputs in charting the history of Indian Islam, and Muslim reformers;

Dr Tahir Mahmood for patiently guiding me through the minefield of Muslim Personal Law and the divisive debate on Uniform Civil Code;

Professors S. Irfan Habib and Amir Ali for their nuanced analysis of the crisis of liberalism among Indian Muslims.

I am also grateful to all those who took time out to share their views on these pages.

However, this book would not have been possible but for my publishers' belief in me—especially Elina Majumdar and Kapish Mehra for commissioning and supporting the project. It was a joy working with their team.

INDEX

1979 Islamic Revolution in Iran 64-65
40 Theses 10
95 Theses 10
aalim fazi 123
Abderrahmani, Kamel 91
Arab Spring 117-18
aggressive majoritarianism 24
Ahle Hadith sect 161
Aijlas 61
Ajlaf 48
Akbar era 55
Akbar, Irena 47
Akhtar, Javed, 29-31
Akyol, Mustafa 70
al-Banna, Hasan 94
Ali, Amir 36-37
Aligarh Muslim University (AMU) 11
Allah 173-74
al-Qaeda 64, 66, 68
al-Qaradawi, Yusuf 96
Ameerul Momineen 154
American secularism 103

Armstrong, Karen, British Islamic scholar 82
Ashrafs 48, 61
Ataturk, Mustafa Kemal 35
Aydin, Mehmet 103
Azad, Maulana Abul Kalam 84, 188-90
Azhar, Masood 123

Babri Masjid 145
Babur 54
Bareilly (Barelvi) school 59
Battle for British Islam, The 120
Bibi, Asia 15, 90-91
Bigamy in Indian practice 139
blasphemy 90
Borker, Hem 86, 87-88

Catholic beliefs 26
Chennai-based Islamic Forum for the Promotion of Moderate Thought 51
Cheraman Juma Masjid 54

Christian European powers 70
Civil society 96
communalist Islam 59
Communist Party of India's women's wing 20-21
conscientious objection 26
Conservative Islam, rise of 57-62
Contrafactual historians 62
Converts, repulsed by the violent forms of Islam 110
Cultural Muslim 6-9
  Jinnah, Mohammad Ali, invoked vision of a secular State 6

Dalwai, Hamid 33-35
de Caen, Sophie 118
Deenar, Malik 54
de-hyphenating liberal and Islam 26
Deoband School 57-58
Deobandi strategy 58
Din-e-Ilahi 59
doctrine of immutability 116

Ex-Muslims 108-9
disingenuous arguments 115

fatwa-spewing mullahs 18
frustrated Muslim youth 81-82
fundamentalist schools 59
fundamentalists 152

Ganga-Jamni tehzeeb 55
Ghettoization 121
Ghubar-e-Khatir 84
global Muslim ummah 66
Guha, Ram Chandra 23
  Hindu-Muslim liberal spectrum 24

Hadiths 127-28
Hamid, Zakri Abdul 122
Hanafi timespan 161
Haqqani, Husain 71-72
Hasan, Saba 21-22
Heretic 121

Hindu communalists 80
Hindu Reform movements 60
Hinduization of nationalist movement 61
Hindu-Muslim Syncretic Shrines and Communities 59
Hindu-Muslim syncretism 58-59
  Bhakti movement and Sufism, interaction between 59
House of Islam, The 89
Husain, Zakir (Dr.) 196-98

Ijma (consensus) 13
Ijtihad 171
India
  constitution 145
  constitutional separation between the State and religion 103
  freedom of worship to all citizens 103
Indian 'Muslim spring 179-80
  informed' Muslims 183
  Islamic theology 85-86
  liberal Muslim reformers 41
  lynch mobs 69
  madrasas 124
India's Muslim Spring: Why Is Nobody Talking About It 39
Indian Islam/Muslim 3
  attitudes towards Sharia or the Muslim Personal Law, decadence and fundamentalism 91
  Ganga-Jamni tehzeeb 47-48
Indian ulema 152
Indian Wahhabi movement of Shah Wali Ullah Dehlavi 57-58
institutional illiberalism 80
Intellectuals in the Modern Islamic World 85
Iqbal, Muhammad Allama 60, 148-49
Iran
  aggressive secularization under Reza Shah Pahlavi 99
IS 64, 66
Islam Without Extremes: A Muslim Case

INDEX

for Liberty 113
Islamic eschatology 151
Islamic fundamentalist authoritarian regimes 98
Islamic Liberal discourse 19, 144
Islamic Renaissance 88
Islamic Revival in British India 58
Islamic Revivalists 171
Islamic rituals 4
Islamic scriptures 69
Islamic State 96
Islamic theology 65
Islamist terror 67
Islamophobia 67, 77

Jalal, Ayesha 6
Jamaat-e-Islami 153
Jamaat-i Islami 61
Jauhar, Maulana Mohammad Ali 191-92
jihadis 64
Jihadism 70-71

Karwan-e-Mohabbat India 44-45
Kellogg–Briand Pact of 1928 156
Khan, Amir's views 48-49
Khan, Maulana Waheeduddin 155-56
Khan, Ovais Sultan 17
Khan, Sir Syed Ahmad 186-88
 Aligarh Movement 187
 Aligarh Muslim University 187-88
 M. A. O. High School 187
 Muhammadan Anglo Oriental College 187
Kharijites/ Islamic State fighters 64
Khilafat agitation 60-61

liberalized Sharia 92
lynch mobs 80

Madrasas and the Making of Islamic Womanhood 86
Mahmood, Tahir 92
mainstream conservatism vs. smattering of Left liberalism 43

Making Sense of Pakistan 6-7
Mander, Harsh 23
Marxist liberals 44
Marxist Muslims 44
Maududi, Abul Ala 94
Maulana 185
Maulana Hasrat Mohani or Syed Fazl-ul-Hasan 193-96
Metcalf, Barbara 58
middle-of-the-road liberals 44
middle-of-the-road *namaazi-parhezgar* 51
moderate Muslims 39, 80
moderate-fundamentalist divide 38-39
modern' Islam, notion of 95
Mohammed Bin Salman (MBS) 75
Moulvis 136-37, 138, 170
Mujeeb, Mohammed (late) 83-84
mullah-Marx narrative 43
mullahs 179
Mumbai-based Bharatiya Muslim Mahila Andolan 51
Muslim Cause 153
Muslim family laws 136-37
Muslim fundamentalists 152-53
Muslim identity
Muslim modernism under Sir Saiyyid Ahmad Khan 60
Muslim Personal Law 22, 34

naam ke mussalman (Muslims only in name) 28
Nomani, Asra 4-5

obscurantist ideology 75-76
Ottoman Empire, destruction of 69, 93
Ottomans 63
Ourghi, Abdel Hakim 10-11
Owaisi, Asaduddin, leader of the right-wing All India Majlis-e-Ittehadul Muslimeen 30

Pakistan
 struggling to reconcile its Islamic

identity 100
Pakistan, long arm of 'Muslimness' 6
Pakistan's blasphemy law 7
Palshikar, Suhas 34
Parsi community 145
Perumal, Cheraman 54
Prophet Mohammed 15
proselytism 110
Protestantism 95-96

Qiyas (human reasoning) 13
Quran 13, 152
Qutb, Sayyid 94

Rahman, Faizur 27
Rahman, Maulvi Habibur 58
Ramzan
   al vida ka roza (the farewell fast) 130
Reconstruction of Religious Thought in Islam 62
Ridda (anti-apostasy) wars 155
Rizvi, Ali A 102, 114
Robinson, Francis 58
Rushdie, Salman 15

Salafism 78
Salafi-Wahhabism 78
Satanic Verses, The 15
Saudi Arabia
   hardline Islamic ideology 73-74
      Saudi-funded madrasas 123
Saudization 77-78
secular Islam / Secularizing Islam 40-41, 180-81
Secular-scepticism 104
self-declared Khalifa Baghdadi 154
Shah, Naseeruddin, uber liberal nominal Muslim 31-32
   backlash from fellow liberal Muslims 45
Shaikh, Farzana 100
Sharia 12, 13, 180
   no-go zone in India 91
   practices justified in 13-14

punishment for blasphemy 38
Shia Islam 68, 141
Shikoh, Dara 55
Soman, Zakia, pro-reform Bharatiya Muslim Mahila Andolan 81
Sonia Gandhi, secular convictions 23
Stranger to History: A Son's Journey Through Muslim Lands 6
Students Islamic Movement of India (SIMI) 77
Sufism 56-57, 59
sulh-i-kul (peace with all) 55, 170
Sunnah (sayings of the Prophet) 13
Sunni 68
   schools of law 139
Sword Verses 157

Tablighi Jam'aat or Preaching society 61
Taliban 64, 123
Taseer, Salman
   as an ostensibly liberal Muslim 8
   as liberal Pakistani politician 7

umma 16
Uniform Civil Code 34
Upanishads 55

Violent Islamic extremism 155
virtue-signalling 128
Vision of Islam 143
vulnerable religious minorities, persecution of 15

Wahhabi Shias 141
Wahhabi/ Salafi Islam 73
Wahhabism 74-75
Walking By Moonlight: My Journey Out Of Islam 111-12
Western Muslim dissidents 182
Wright, Robin 95

young Muslims, crisis of faith 106

Zakaullah 55